A VISUAL GUIDE TO
SPACE EXPLORATION

Rosen
YA

ALBERTO HERNÁNDEZ PAMPLONA

This edition published in 2018 by
The Rosen Publishing Group, Inc.
29 East 21st Street
New York, NY 10010

Library of Congress Cataloging-in-Publication Data

Names: Pamplona, Alberto Hernández, author.
Title: A visual guide to space exploration / Alberto Hernández Pamplona.
Description: New York : Rosen Publishing, 2018 | Series: A visual exploration of science | Audience: Grades 7–12. | Includes bibliographic references and index.
Identifiers: LCCN 2017002112 | ISBN 9781508175834 (library-bound)
Subjects: LCSH: Astronomy—History—Juvenile literature. | Outer space—Exploration—Juvenile literature. | Outer space—Exploration—History—Juvenile literature
Classification: LCC QB46 .P25 2018 | DDC 629.43/5—dc23
LC record available at https://lccn.loc.gov/2017002112

Manufactured in the United States of America

Metric Conversion Chart

1 inch = 2.54 centimeters; 25.4 millimeters
1 foot = 30.48 centimeters
1 yard = .914 meters
1 square foot = .093 square meters
1 square mile = 2.59 square kilometers
1 ton = .907 metric tons
1 pound = 454 grams
1 mile = 1.609 kilometers
1 cup = 250 milliliters

1 ounce = 28 grams
1 fluid ounce = 30 milliliters
1 teaspoon = 5 milliliters
1 tablespoon = 15 milliliters
1 quart = .946 liters
355 degrees F = 180 degrees Celsius

Original Idea Sol90 Publishing
Project Manegement Nuria Cicero
Editorial Coordination Diana Malizia
Editorial Team Alberto Hernández, Virginia Iris Fernández, Mar Valls, Marta de la Serna, Sebastián Romeu. Maximiliano Ludueña, Carlos Bodyadjan, Doris Elsa Bustamante, Tania Domenicucci, Andrea Giacobone, Constanza Guariglia, Joaquín Hidalgo, Hernán López Winne.
Proofreaders Marta Kordon, Edgardo D'Elio
Design Fabián Cassan
Layout Laura Ocampo, Carolina Berdiñas, Clara Miralles, Paola Fornasaro, Mariana Marx, Pablo Alarcón

Photography Age Fotostock, Getty Images, Science Photo Library, Graphic News, ESA, NASA, National Geographic, Latinstock, Album, ACI, Cordon Press

Infographic Coordination Paula López

Infographies Sol90 Images www.sol90images.com , Paula López, Guillermina Eichel, Pablo Gentile, Maru Hiriart, Maureen Holboll, Clarisa Mateo, Sol Molina, Vanina Ogueta, Gastón Pérsico, Cecilia Szalkowicz, Paula Simonetti

Illustrations Sol90 Images www.sol90images.com , Guido Arroyo, Pablo Aschei, Gustavo J. Caironi, Hernán Cañellas, Leonardo César, José Luis Corsetti, Vanina Farías, Joana Garrido, Celina Hilbert, Isidro López, Diego Martín, Jorge Martínez, Marco Menco, Ala de Mo Diego Mourelos, Eduardo Pérez, Javier Pérez, Ariel Piroyansky, Ariel Roldán, Marcel Socías, Néstor Taylor, Trebol Animation, Juan Venegas, Coralia Vignau, 3DN, 3DOM studio, Constanza Vicco, Diego Mourelos.

Contents

A Voyage into the Future

During the greater part of our history, the Moon was quite unreachable. It did not seem very big and far away but rather small. For the Greeks, the idea of walking on the Moon was certainly unthinkable, and as recently as the end of the 19th century many people doubted that humans would even be able to fly. Nevertheless, on July 20, 1969, the miracle happened. Since then many historic missions to explore the planets have been planned and executed, with the spacecraft and probes Mariner, Viking, Pioneer, Voyager, and Galileo leading the way. Thanks to human intelligence and effort we have succeeded in exploring many corners of our solar system. This book intends to show all this: the history of manned and unmanned voyages and the discoveries that were made. We will try, using simple and accessible language, to answer many questions, such as what rockets are, how they work, what shuttles exist, how astronauts live in space, and which robot probes are visiting other planets looking for signs of life. All this is accompanied by photographs and top-quality illustrations, providing a better picture of the successes by which we have made giant steps in our understanding of the composition of the other planets, their origin, and their evolution. Every day astronomers are more convinced that there are other places in the universe that are like Earth. We only have to find them. They also assure us that this is one of the most interesting moments in the exploration of the solar

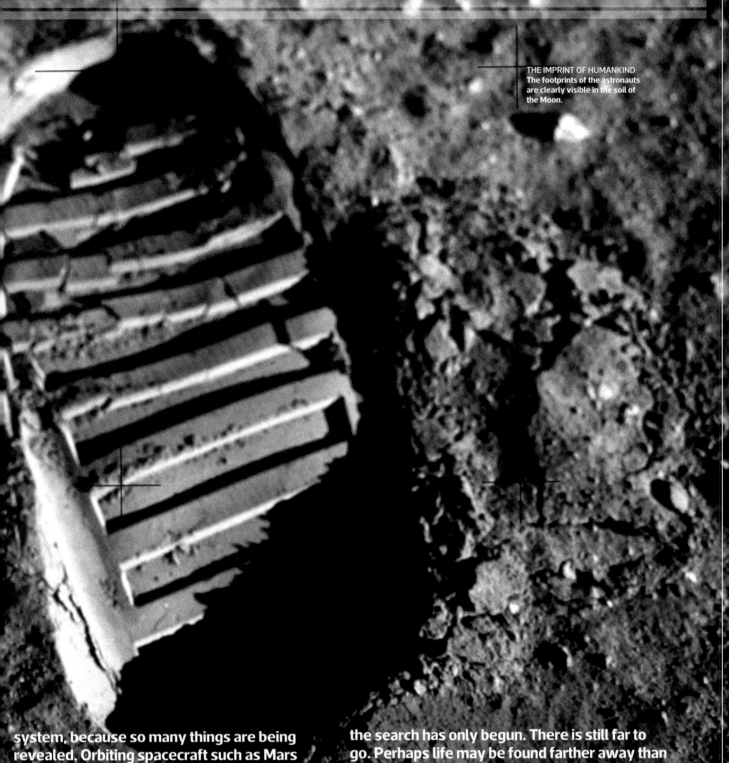

THE IMPRINT OF HUMANKIND
The footprints of the astronauts are clearly visible in the soil of the Moon.

system, because so many things are being revealed. Orbiting spacecraft such as Mars Odyssey and Mars Express have confirmed the existence of ice under the surface of Mars. Sending exploratory spacecraft to Saturn was another prodigious feat, a demonstration of human capacity to dream of new worlds. In 2015, the New Horizons space probe became the first craft to do an exploratory flyby of Pluto. This shows that the search has only begun. There is still far to go. Perhaps life may be found farther away than we had imagined. Or maybe, as some dreamers imagine, in the next decade we will realize the project of colonizing other planets. For now, the best candidate for us to land on is Mars. But that is still only a dream, the same kind of dream that was made into reality when humans left their footprints on the Moon.

The Conquest of Space

The human adventure in space began with Yuri Gagarin, the first Russian astronaut, who in 1961 reached an altitude of 196 miles (315 km) and orbited the Earth in the spacecraft Vostok 1. The cosmonaut had practically no control over the apparatus, which was remotely controlled by Soviet engineers. The next step was made by the United States with

he arrival of astronauts on the Moon. Neil Armstrong became the first man o set foot on the Moon, followed by Edwin Aldrin. The success of the Apollo 1 mission marked the culmination of a long and costly space project whose objective was to explore Earth's only natural satellite. In the following decades, the space program has had many significant successes. ●

Destination: Other Worlds

The space age began in 1957 with the launching of the first artificial satellite. Since that time, astronauts and space probes have left the Earth to investigate space. To date, 12 men have visited the Moon. Advances in astronautics have made it possible to develop automatic navigational systems with which a spacecraft can reach and enter orbit around a planet. The Mars Express probe, launched in 2003 to take photographs of Mars, used this system. Mars Express, one of the European Space Agency's most productive missions around the Red Planet, is powered exclusively by solar energy.

Automatic Navigational System

Spacecraft that are unmanned, such as the artificial satellites that orbit planets, transmit their information to Earth using radio equipment. The area of satellite coverage depends on the type of orbit. There are also probes that touch down on the surface, as was the case with Venus, Mars, and the Moon. The real work begins when the apparatus reaches its target. The instruments are activated to gather data that are sent to Earth for analysis.

SOLAR PANEL
Provides energy
for navigation

FUEL TANKS
70 gallons
(270 l) of
propellant each

THRUSTER
Used to correct
the orbit

CONVENTIONAL NAVIGATION

During the encounter, Earth-based optical navigation is limited by the time it takes a radio signal to reach the spacecraft.

Navigational systems based on Earth require radio tracking.

The images taken are transmitted to Earth, and the navigational commands are sent to the spacecraft.

2 The probe deploys its solar panels and begins its own life running on solar energy. It sends signals to Earth to check that its instruments are working properly.

LAUNCH

Maneuvers are calculated on Earth, and the parameters are transmitted to the spacecraft.

LAUNCH

1 On June 2, 2003, the Mars Express probe left Earth on a Soyuz rocket launched from Kazakhstan. Once it escaped Earth's orbit, the probe activated its Fregat boosters and began its path toward the orbit of Mars.

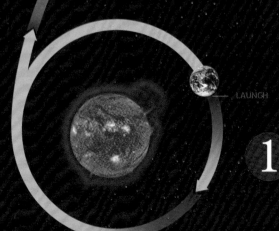

4 The transmission of data to Earth is carried out when the probe is at the maximum height of its orbit around Mars. At that moment, the high-gain antenna turns away from the Red Planet to aim toward the Earth. Mars Express began orbiting Mars in December 2003.

HIGH-GAIN ANTENNA
For long-distance communication with Earth

3 Mars Express begins its voyage toward Mars, which would last almost seven months. The probe is monitored from Mission Control Center in Darmstadt, Germany. Communication with the probe is done by radio. To avoid colliding with Mars, the Mars Express corrects its trajectory.

Space Programs

The voyages are planned years in advance. Space probes are automatic vehicles that can use the gravitational field of one planet to reach another. Some only pass at a preset distance from the planet they are studying; others (orbiters) follow a route that places them in planetary orbit. From there they can send smaller landing probes, which deploy data-collecting instruments. Manned spacecraft, however, require designs that include air, water, food, seats, and rest areas, as well as navigation-, control-, and information-transmission equipment.

UNMANNED

12 feet
(3.7 m)

ARTIFICIAL SATELLITE IN POLAR ORBIT
Nimbus

89 feet
(27 m)

METEOROLOGICAL SATELLITE
GOES

17 feet
(5.1 m)

FLYBY SPACE PROBE
Mariner

4.3 feet
(1.3 m)

ORBITING SPACE PROBE
Galileo

11 feet
(3.3 m)

PROBE WITH A LANDING DEVICE
Viking

1 foot
(0.3 m)

EXPLORATION VEHICLE
Sojourner

SPACE WALK

To gather more information, the astronauts conduct a space walk outside the spacecraft.

MANNED

5 feet
(1.5 m)

VOSTOK PROGRAM
Vostok 1

57.4 feet
(17.5 m)

APOLLO PROGRAM
Apollo 11

11.5 feet
(3.4 m)

GEMINI PROGRAM
Gemini 8

56 feet
(17 m)

SPACE SHUTTLE
Columbia

115 feet
(35 m)

SPACE STATION
Mir

49 feet
(15 m)

SPACE STATION
Skylab

From Fiction to Reality

Astronautics was born toward the end of the 19th century, when the Russian Konstantin Tsiolkovsky foresaw the ability of a rocket to overcome the force of gravity. Other pioneers were Hermann Oberth, who designed a liquid–fueled missile in 1917, which was later built by the American Robert Goddard in 1926. The German Wernher von Braun built the Redstone, Jupiter, and Saturn rockets, which made the manned landing on the Moon possible. Astronautics officially began in 1957 with the launching of the first artificial satellite, Sputnik 1. The second was Sputnik 2, which had on board the dog Laika. ●

Sputnik 1

inaugurated the period of Russian supremacy in the so–called space race. Sputnik 1, launched in 1957, was an aluminum sphere 23 inches (58 cm) in diameter. It had instrumentation that sent back information about cosmic radiation, meteorites, and the density and temperature of the Earth's upper atmosphere for 21 days. It was destroyed by aerodynamic friction when it reentered the atmosphere 57 days later.

THE SECOND

Robert Goddard designed a rocket 10 feet (3 m) high. After ignition, it rose 40 feet (12 m) and then crashed 184 feet (56 m) away.

THE FIRST

In Germany, Hermann Oberth designed a liquid–fueled missile in 1917 that would promote the idea of spaceflight.

THE THIRD

Wernher von Braun, working for NASA, was the creator of the Saturn V rocket, which carried astronauts to the Moon a number of times between 1969 and 1972.

Robert Goddard
1882–1945
The US physicist studied rockets and demonstrated their use for space travel.

Hermann Oberth
1894–1989
The scientist who worked on rocket technology during World War II.

Wernher von Braun
1912–1977
The German physicist worked for Adolf Hitler designing ballistic missiles.

SPUTNIK 1

Launch	October 1957
Orbital altitude	370 miles (600 km)
Orbital period	97 minutes
Weight	184 pounds (83.6 kg)
Country	USSR

1609
GALILEO
constructed the first astronomical telescope and observed the craters on the moon.

1798
CAVENDISH
demonstrated that the law of gravity applies to all bodies.

1806
ROCKETS
The first military rockets were invented. They were used in an aerial attack in 1814.

1838
DISTANCE
The distance to the star 61 Cygni was measured, using the Earth's orbit as a baseline.

1926
THE FIRST ROCKET
Robert Goddard launched the first liquid-fueled rocke

With a Dog

Sputnik 2 was the second satellite launched into Earth's orbit by the Russians (on Nov. 3, 1957) and the first one to carry a living creature, the dog Laika. The satellite was 13 feet (4 m) long and 6 feet (2 m) in diameter. The dog was connected to a machine that registered her vital signs, and oxygen was provided to her by an air regeneration system. Food and water were dispensed in the form of a gelatin.

SPUTNIK 2

Launch	November 1957
Orbital altitude	1,030 miles (1,660 km)
Orbital period	103.7 minutes
Weight	1,118 pounds (508 kg)
Country	USSR

WEIGHT ON EARTH

1,118 pounds
(508 kg)

DIMENSIONS
Sputnik 2 was 13 feet (4 m) long and 6 feet (2 m) in diameter at the base.

SPUTNIK 2

The canine passenger was protected by a pressurized cabin.

- Aerodynamic nose
- Mechanism for ejection from the nose
- Scientific instruments
- Support structure
- Radio transmitter
- Pressurized cabin
- Heat shield
- Fan
- Safety ring
- Retrothrusters
- Telecommunications antenna

PASSENGER
The dog Laika was the first to visit space.

Explorer 1

The United States independently developed its first satellite, Explorer 1, which was launched from Cape Canaveral in 1958. The satellite was a cylinder 6 inches (15 cm) in diameter; it weighed 31 pounds (14 kg) and measured cosmic radiation and meteorites for 112 days, which led to the discovery of the Van Allen belts. It was designed and constructed by the Jet Propulsion Laboratory of the California Institute of Technology.

EXPLORER 1

Launch	Jan./Feb. 1958
Orbital altitude	1,580 miles (2,550 km)
Orbital period	114.8 minutes
Weight	31 pounds (14 kg)
Organization	NASA

WEIGHT ON EARTH

31 pounds
(14 kg)

DIMENSIONS
Explorer 1 weighed 31 pounds (14 kg) and was 2.6 feet (0.8 m) high and 6 inches (15 cm) in diameter.

PIECE BY PIECE

Explorer 1 was designed by NASA in 1958.

- Cable antenna
- Micrometeorite detectors
- Conical nose cone
- High-gain transmitter
- Internal temperature indicator
- Fiberglass ring

WEIGHT ON THE EARTH

184 pounds
(83.6 kg)

ANTENNAS
Sputnik 1 had four antennas between 7.9 and 9.5 feet (2.4–2.9 m) long.

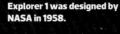

1927
n July 5 the German ssociation for aceflight was formed.

1932
began his investigations on rockets for the German military.

1936
Guggenheim Aeronautical Laboratory. Later its name was changed to the Jet Propulsion Laboratory.

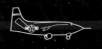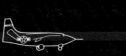

1947
Chuck Yeager broke the sound barrier aboard the rocket plane X–1.

1949
The first stage of a two-stage rocket, which reached an altitude of 244 miles (393 km)

1957
On October 4 the Soviet Union launched the Sputnik 1 satellite into space.

NASA Yesterday and Today

NA

The National Aeronautics and Space Administration (NASA) is the agency that organized the US space program. It was created in 1958 as part of the space race with the then Soviet Union. It planned all national activities linked with space exploration. It has a launch center (the Kennedy Space Center) and other installations all over the country. ●

NASA Centers

NASA's activities in astronautics and space research are so numerous and so varied that it has different complexes all over the United States. The agency has a number of installations for research, flight simulation, astronaut training, and preparation. NASA's headquarters are in Washington, D.C., and the Mission Control Center is in Houston. Another important center is the Jet Propulsion Laboratory, whose responsibilities include managing the Deep Space Network, which maintains constant communication with space missions through its facilities in California, Spain, and Australia.

Indian River

AMES RESEARCH CENTER
Founded in 1939, it is the experimental base for many missions. It is equipped with flight simulators and advanced technology.

JOHNSON SPACE CENTER
Astronauts are selected and trained at the Houston center. Spaceflight takeoffs and landings are controlled from here.

MARSHALL SPACE FLIGHT CENTER
manages the transport of equipment, the propulsion systems, and the launching of the space shuttle.

VISITOR'S CENTER

GLENN RESEARCH CENTER

INDEPENDENT VERIFICATION AND VALIDATION FACILITY

GODDARD INSTITUTE FOR SPACE STUDIES

NASA CONTROL CENTER WASHINGTON, D.C.

WALLOPS FLIGHT FACILITY

LANGLEY RESEARCH CENTER

WHITE SANDS TEST CENTER

KENNEDY SPACE CENTER

MICHOUD ASSEMBLY FACILITY

OTHER DEEP SPACE CENTERS

JET PROPULSION LABORATORY
designs flight systems and provides technical assessment. Directs the Deep Space Network.

ARMSTRONG FLIGHT RESEARCH CENTER
is involved in atmosphere-related activities. It has been in operation since 1947.

GODDARD SPACE FLIGHT CENTER
designs, manufactures, and monitors scientific satellites to investigate the Earth and other planets.

MADRID DEEP SPACE COMMUNICATIONS COMPLEX

CANBERRA DEEP SPA COMMUNICATION COMPLEX

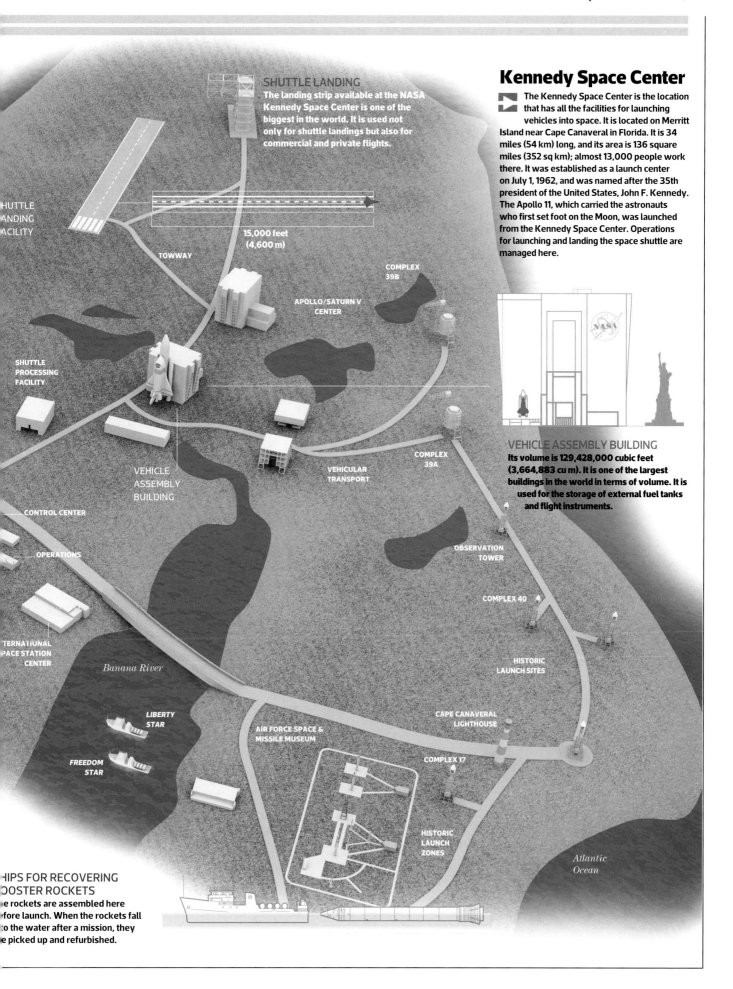

SHUTTLE LANDING
The landing strip available at the NASA Kennedy Space Center is one of the biggest in the world. It is used not only for shuttle landings but also for commercial and private flights.

SHUTTLE LANDING FACILITY

15,000 feet (4,600 m)

TOWWAY

COMPLEX 39B

APOLLO/SATURN V CENTER

SHUTTLE PROCESSING FACILITY

VEHICLE ASSEMBLY BUILDING

CONTROL CENTER

OPERATIONS

VEHICULAR TRANSPORT

COMPLEX 39A

INTERNATIONAL SPACE STATION CENTER

Banana River

LIBERTY STAR

FREEDOM STAR

AIR FORCE SPACE & MISSILE MUSEUM

OBSERVATION TOWER

COMPLEX 40

HISTORIC LAUNCH SITES

CAPE CANAVERAL LIGHTHOUSE

COMPLEX 17

HISTORIC LAUNCH ZONES

Atlantic Ocean

Kennedy Space Center

The Kennedy Space Center is the location that has all the facilities for launching vehicles into space. It is located on Merritt Island near Cape Canaveral in Florida. It is 34 miles (54 km) long, and its area is 136 square miles (352 sq km); almost 13,000 people work there. It was established as a launch center on July 1, 1962, and was named after the 35th president of the United States, John F. Kennedy. The Apollo 11, which carried the astronauts who first set foot on the Moon, was launched from the Kennedy Space Center. Operations for launching and landing the space shuttle are managed here.

VEHICLE ASSEMBLY BUILDING
Its volume is 129,428,000 cubic feet (3,664,883 cu m). It is one of the largest buildings in the world in terms of volume. It is used for the storage of external fuel tanks and flight instruments.

SHIPS FOR RECOVERING BOOSTER ROCKETS
The rockets are assembled here before launch. When the rockets fall into the water after a mission, they are picked up and refurbished.

Other Space Agencies

T he activity of exploring the cosmos was increased in 1975 with the creation of the European Space Agency (ESA). This intergovernmental organization is second only to NASA in its investment in space. The Mir space station, launched by the Russian Space Agency (RKA), remained in Earth orbit for 15 years and was a milestone for living in space. Other agencies, such as the Canadian Space Agency (CSA) and the Japanese Space Agency (JAXA), also made technological contributions to the exploration of the Earth's orbit and the solar system. ●

KOUROU, FRENCH GUIANA
EUROPEAN LAUNCHING BASE

Latitude: 5° north, 300 miles (500 km) north of the Equator. Close to the Equator, which is an advantage for rockets in reaching Earth's orbit. The region is almost unpopulated and free from earthquakes.

Surface area	285 square miles (750 sq km)
Total cost	1,600 million euros
First operation	1968 (as a French base)
Employees	1,525

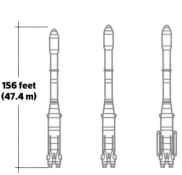

EUROPEAN SPACE AGENCY

Founded	1975
Members	22
Current Budget	5.25 billion euros ($5.77 billion)
Employees	2,000

KEY

■ Members of the European Space Agency

Europe in Space

► The ESA was formed as a single organization in 1975 by the fusion of the European Space Research Organization (ESRO) and the European Launcher Development Organization (ELDO). It carried out important missions, such as Venus Express, Mars Express, and Ulysses (with which NASA also participated). Nineteen percent of the ESA's annual budget goes into the construction of launch vehicles.

THE ARIANE FAMILY

The development of the Ariane rocket made the ESA a leader in the space-launch market. Ariane was chosen for satellites from Japanese, Canadian, and American companies.

156 feet (47.4 m)

Ariane 1   Ariane 2   Ariane 3   Ariane 4   Ariane 5   Ariane 5 evolution

Mission Threshold

The ESA concentrated a great effort on the Planck mission from 2009 to 2013. The mission was launched with the hope that it would establish the precise age of the universe and test different expansion models. It also sought to improve on the results from the US WMAP mission on the formation and evolution of the universe and the background cosmic radiation. Planck had 10 times better resolution than WMAP. The launch took place in 2009 using an Ariane rocket. The mission lasted a total of four years and provided scientists with important data that was released in a full mission report in 2014.

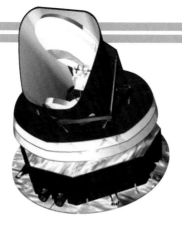

PLANCK MISSION

Launch year	2009
Mission duration	4 years, 5 months
Launch vehicle	Ariane 5
Weight at launch	4,300 lb (1,950 kg)

Canadian Space Agency

The CSA was created in 1990, although it had prior involvement in astronautic activities. The first Canadian launch occurred in 1962 with the Alouette 1 satellite. The most important work of the CSA is Radarsat, launched in November 1995. It provides information about the environment and is used in cartography, hydrology, oceanography, and agriculture. The Canadian agency also participated in the International Space Station (ISS) by providing the robot arm called the Mobile Service System (MSS).

Japanese Space Agency

On October 1, 2003, three independent organizations were combined to form the JAXA: the Institute of Space and Astronautical Science (ISAS), the National Aerospace Laboratory (NAL), and the National Space Development Agency (NASDA). Its most outstanding mission is the Hayabusa, launched in May 2003 as the first mission designed to land on an asteroid. It reached the asteroid Itokawa in November 2005. Despite problems with the probe, it returned to Earth in 2010 with samples taken from the surface of the asteroid.

Russian Federal Space Agency

Formed after the dissolution of the Soviet Union, it uses the technology and launching sites that it inherited from the Soviet space program. The Russian agency was responsible for orbiting the Mir space station, the direct predecessor of the International Space Station. Mir was assembled in orbit after separate launches of different modules between 1986 and 1996. It was destroyed in a controlled manner at the end of its useful life on March 23, 2001.

РОСКОСМОС

TRANSPORT ROUTE

TOWARD THE FINAL DESIGN
The rocket goes to the assembly building for final details.

ASSEMBLY BUILDING
Once the process is complete, the rocket is transferred to the platform.

LAUNCH PLATFORM
After covering 2 miles (3.5 km) at 2 mph (3.5 km/h), the Ariane is ready for liftoff.

MIR STATION
housed the cosmonauts and astronauts in space.

PROGRESS-M
used to supply food and fuel.

USEFUL LIFE
15 years

SOLAR PANELS
supply the station with electricity from solar energy.

PRINCIPAL MODULE
used as living quarters and general control of the station.

SOYUZ ROCKET
The rocket of the Russian agency that is used to put spacecraft into orbit.

Russian Missions

After the initial successes with small satellites, where the effect of weightlessness was tested on animals, the Soviet Union, like the United States, began to develop programs for launching human beings into space. The first astronaut to orbit the Earth, at an altitude of 196 miles (315 km), was Yuri Gagarin in 1961. He was the sole crew member of the Russian spacecraft Vostok 1. Gagarin orbited the Earth in his capsule, which was lifted into orbit by the SL-3 rocket and which had an ejection system for the cosmonaut in case of emergency. ●

Russians in Space

In Vostok 1 the cosmonaut had practically no control over the spacecraft, which was controlled remotely by Soviet engineers. The spacecraft consisted of a spherical cabin weighing 2.46 tons with a diameter of 7.5 feet (2.3 m). The single-person cabin was mounted on the module, which contained the rocket engine. Yuri Gagarin's reentry was done with parachutes.

VOSTOK 1

Launch	April 1961
Orbital altitude	196 miles (315 km)
Orbital period	1 hour, 48 min
Weight	5,400 pounds (2,460 kg)
Organization	U.S.S.R.

THE FIRST
On board Vostok 1, Gagarin was the first person to go into space. In 1961 he orbited the Earth at an altitude of 196 miles (315 km).

Yuri Gagarin
1934-68
The Russian cosmonaut helped in promoting Russian astronautics. He died in a routine flight, on board a MiG-15 jet.

THE FIRST WOMAN
She traveled into space on board the Vostok 6 in 1963. During that mission, she flew 48 orbits around the Earth in 71 hours of flight.

Valentina Tereshkova
(b. 1937)
Tereshkova was a parachute jumping enthusiast. It was not until 19 years later that another woman became a cosmonaut.

A WALK IN SPACE
Leonov was the first to perform a space walk. In March 1965 the spacecraft Voshkod 2 carried him to outer space.

Aleksey A. Leonov
(b. 1934)
In 1953 he joined the Air Force and in 1959 began training for spaceflight. In 1975 he commanded the Apollo-Soyuz mission.

WEIGHT ON EARTH
11,000 pounds
(5,000 kg)

15 feet (4.5 m)

ANTENNAS
It had powerful antennas to stay in contact with the Earth.

PART BY PART
Diagram of the Vostok with each of its components

Inflatable air lock

Nitrogen and oxygen storage tanks

Access port

VHS antenna

Motor controls

Retrothruster

1957
SPUTNIK 2
On November 3 the second Soviet satellite was launched, with the dog Laika.

1958
EXPLORER 1
First American satellite to orbit the Earth. It was launched in February.

1958
NASA
The National Aeronautics and Space Administration was founded in the United States.

1959
LUNA 1
Launched by the Soviet Union in January, it came within 3,500 miles (6,000 km) of the Moon.

1959
LUNA 3
Launched in October, it took photos of the far side of the Moon.

1960
LITTLE DOGS
Strelka and Belka returned alive from a trip in orbit that lasted one day.

From Russia with Love

Vostok ("east" in Russian) was a Soviet spacecraft program that put six cosmonauts into orbit around the Earth between April 1961 and June 1963. On June 16, 1963, a manned spacecraft of the series lifted off carrying the first female cosmonaut in the world, Valentina Tereshkova. This was a joint flight with Vostok 5, piloted by Valery Bykovsky. During this mission, medical and biological investigations were carried out, and various matters related to systems development of the spacecraft were analyzed. The spacecraft are still being used today, sending cosmonauts to the International Space Station.

VOSTOK PROGRAM

MISSIONS

Vostok 1	April 12, 1961
Vostok 2	Aug. 6, 1961
Vostok 3	Aug. 11, 1962
Vostok 4	Aug. 12, 1962
Vostok 5	June 14, 1963
Vostok 6	June 16, 1963

Nitrogen storage tank

Cosmonaut

smonaut ction seat

VOSTOK BOOSTER ROCKET

To be able to leave the Earth, Vostok needed a booster rocket.

Manned module

FIRST STAGE   SECOND STAGE   THIRD STAGE

VOSTOK BOOSTER ROCKET

Vostok was the first mission that carried a human into space, the cosmonaut Yuri Gagarin.

1 The spacecraft was launched from the cosmodrome in Baikonur, in Tyuratam, at 9:07 A.M.

Liftoff

2 Separation occurred at 10:25, and the cosmonaut's reentry began at 10:35.

3 The cosmonaut ejects from the rocket with a parachute.

4 The cosmonaut separates himself from the ejection seat at an altitude of 13,000 feet (4,000 m).

5 The cosmonaut lands in Saratov at 11:05 A.M.

Return Ticket

The flight began in Tyuratam, rising to an altitude of 196 miles (315 km). First it crossed a part of Siberia and then the entire breadth of the Pacific Ocean; it passed between Cape Horn and Antarctica, and once it had crossed the Atlantic it flew in African skies over the Congo. The capsule with Gagarin separated from the launch rocket (which continued in orbit) and began its descent. It landed in Saratov, approximately 460 miles (740 km) east of Moscow.

61
AM
e first chimpanzee
e sent into space
a suborbital flight

1961
VOSTOK 1
In a flight of 108 minutes, the Russian Yuri Gagarin orbits the Earth.

1961
MERCURY
NASA's Alan Shepard made a suborbital flight of 15 minutes.

1964
GEMINI 1
The first two Gemini were launched as unmanned flights in 1964 and 1965.

1964
VOSHKOD 1
A crew of three went into space for the first time.

1965
VOSHKOD 2
Aleksey Leonov succeeded in leaving the spacecraft and carried out the first space walk.

North American Spacecraft

Over the course of the space race between the Soviet Union and the United States, the United States developed the Mercury program between 1959 and 1963. The manned capsule was small, with a volume of only 60 cubic feet (1.7 cu m). Before the first manned mission in May 1961, the American project sent three monkeys into space. The Mercury spacecraft was launched into space by two rockets: the Redstone, used for suborbital flights, and the Atlas, which was used in the five orbital flights that were achieved. Little Joe was used to test the escape tower and controls for aborting a mission.

Mercury Spacecraft
- Escape tower
- Manned module
- Fuel tank

Launch rocket
- Oxidant tank
- Motor

THRUSTERS

HEAT SHIELD

DOUBLE WALL

The Mercury Experience

The development of the mission hardware was more a product of politics than of scientific intent. After the launching of Sputnik 1 in 1957 and within the framework of the Cold War, the United States made efforts to start its own space program. The development of the Mercury spacecraft was the initial step for getting the Apollo project off the ground. It was announced as a mission to fly past the Moon in 1961 but was changed by President Kennedy because he wanted an American to reach the Moon, set foot on it, and return home.

TESTING
The first sentient beings in space were animals, sent in order to ensure that humans could survive spaceflight.

Ham
was the first monkey to fly into space. The spacecraft had sensors and remote-control instruments; Ham survived life in space without problems.

THE FIRST
On May 5, 1961, Shepard lifted off from Cape Canaveral and became the first American to fly on board a Mercury spacecraft.

Alan Shepard
1923–98
After his first voyage into space, he held important positions with NASA. In 1971 he was part of the Apollo 14 mission.

THE LAST
He was commander of the last Mercury mission, which in May 1963 completed 22 orbits and closed the operational phase of the project.

Gordon Cooper
1927–2004
Selected as an astronaut in 1959. In 1965 he carried out a Gemini mission that lasted 190 hours and 56 minutes. He retired in 1970.

WEIGHT ON EARTH

4,257 pounds
(1,935 kg)

MODULE
The height of the Mercury capsule is scarcely greater than the height of the average person.

MERCURY

TECHNICAL SPECIFICATIONS

1st launch	July 29, 1960
Maximum altitude	175 miles (282 km)
Diameter	6 feet (2 m)
Maximum duration	22 orbits (34 hours)
Organization	NASA

1965
MARINER 4
Mariner 4 flew past Mars and took the first photos of the Red Planet.

1965
GEMINI 3
The astronauts Virgil (Gus) Grissom and John Young began the manned flights of this program.

1965
RENDEZVOUS
Gemini 6 and 7 succeeded at completing a rendezvous in space. Gemini was the preceding project to Apollo.

1966
LUNA 9
On February 3 the first landing on the Moon took place. Photos were taken and sent back to Earth.

1966
SURVEYOR 1
The first American Moon landing on June 2. More than 10,000 high-resolution photos were transmitted.

1966
LUNA 10
In April the Soviet Union deployed another satellite that sent radio signals to Earth.

THE VOYAGE

During the flight, the crew had more than 100 controls available. They were also able to see out through a small window.

HELMET

Escape Tower

Tower

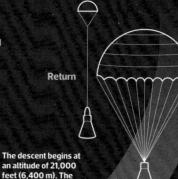

Capsule

OBSERVATION WINDOW

2 Separating from the escape tower and the booster engine, the escape rockets ignite and the parachute system is armed.

Booster Engine

Reentry Parachutes

Capsule

3 The capsule turns 180°. Depending on the mission, it can complete 1–22 orbits. Then the descent begins.

1 With the fuel providing the thrust, the launch vehicle deploys together with the command module. The spacecraft has three solid fuel rockets.

First Voyages

The six successful flights of the Mercury mission used a solid-fuel rocket. The first, a suborbital flight in May 1961, lasted 15 minutes. Over the years, the length of space flights increased thanks to improvements in the spacecraft.

Return

CONTROL PANEL

THRUSTERS

BOOSTERS

AERODYNAMIC ADJUSTMENT

4 The descent begins at an altitude of 21,000 feet (6,400 m). The capsule begins reentry. The parachutes open.

Principal Parachutes

PARACHUTES

Falling into the Ocean

RESCUE ROCKET

5 Before the retrieval, the pilot's parachute and the reserve parachute are detached; they fall into the sea and are retrieved.

MERCURY FLIGHTS

MERCURY WITH ANIMALS

Little Joe	Dec 4, 1959	Sam
Redstone	Jan. 31, 1961	Ham
Atlas 7	Nov. 29, 1961	Enos

MERCURY WITH ASTRONAUTS

Redstone 3	May 5, 1961	Alan Shepard	Freedom 7
Redstone 4	July 21, 1961	Gus Grissom	Liberty Bell 7
Atlas 6	Feb. 20, 1962	John Glenn	Friendship 7
Atlas 7	May 24, 1962	Scott Carpenter	Aurora 7
Atlas 8	Oct. 3, 1962	Wally Schirra	Sigma 7
Atlas 9	May 15, 1963	Gordon Cooper	Faith 7

1966 APOLLO PROGRAM
The Apollo program began in February 1966 with the objective of landing on the Moon.

1967 TRAGEDY
In January three astronauts died in a fire during a routine test of the Apollo program.

1967 SOYUZ 1
The Soviet program also experienced a fatal accident. On April 24, Vladimir Komarov died when his spacecraft crashed while landing.

1968 APOLLO 8
The Saturn V is used for the first time as a booster. Apollo 8 orbits the Moon ten times in six days.

1969 SOYUZ 4 AND 5
The Russian space program successfully docks two spacecraft as Gemini had done.

1969 APOLLO 11
The United States reaches its objective. Edwin Aldrin and Neil Armstrong walk on the Moon.

A Giant Leap

The acceleration of the space race between the United States and the Soviet Union reached its height when President Kennedy's words set the goal of landing on the Moon before the end of the 1960s. This goal was met in 1969 when a human being walked on the Moon for the first time in history. The mission took over a week, including the trip and the stay on the Moon. It was the first launch to use two boosters: one for leaving Earth to get to the Moon and the other to return from the Moon. Neil Armstrong was the first person to leave a human footprint and place a US flag in outer space.

DOCKING RADAR ANTENNA

CABIN

BOOSTER ASSEMBLY CONTROL

EXIT PLATFORM

OXIDANT TANK

EQUIPMENT FOR EXPERIMENTS

LIFTOFF

The module is powered by a Saturn V rocket. With a weight of over 6 million pounds (3 million kg), it was the heaviest rocket that had ever been built.

Launching Platform

1 In 2 minutes and 42 seconds, the rocket reaches a velocity of 6,100 mph (9,800 km/h) and enters Earth's orbit.

Stage 1

Revolution

Stage 3

Modules Joined

3 The orbital and lunar modules stay together.

LUNAR MODULE EAGLE

was divided into two sections, one for ascent and one for descent. It was coupled to the orbital module during the ascent and descent.

WEIGHT ON EARTH

54,000 pounds (24,500 kg)

The Voyage

The total mission to the Moon and back lasted almost 200 hours. For the voyage, two modules were used: the orbital module (*Columbia*) and the lunar module (*Eagle*). Both were attached to the Saturn V rocket until after the third stage. The *Eagle* module, with two astronauts onboard, was separated after making a 180° course correction that placed it in lunar orbit. Then, having been separated, the module fired up its engine and prepared for landing on the Moon. The return trip began on July 24. The stay on the Moon lasted 21 hours and 38 minutes.

2 One revolution is made around the Earth. The second stage is jettisoned, and the ship's velocity reaches 14,620 mph (23,000 km/h).

SATURN V
The rocket that launched Apollo into orbit was as high as a 29-story building.

4 Once lunar orbit is reached, the Eagle module separates and prepares for landing on the Moon.

Module

Correction

LM-5 EAGLE

Landing	July 20, 1969
Height	21 feet (6.5 m)
Cabin volume	235 cubic feet (6.65 cu m)
Crew	2
Organization	NASA

The Modules

The Apollo 11 mission had a spacecraft divided into two parts: the command module *Columbia* and a lunar module, the *Eagle*. Initially they were joined together. When orbit was reached, the lunar module separated to complete its descent and land on the Moon.

ORBITAL MODULE

The use of two modules allowed for a crew of two in the cabin.

MANEUVERABLE ANTENNA

OXYGEN TANKS FOR THRUST

ULTRA HIGH-FREQUENCY ANTENNA

FUEL TANK

LANDING GEAR

ENORMOUS EAGLE
The astronaut is just over one half as tall as the leg of the module.

COMMAND MODULE

SERVICE MODULE

High-Gain Antenna

Thrust Control

Reserve Fuel

Motor

Cabin for the Crew

Fuel Tanks

Propulsion System

Two Tanks of Helium

CSM-107 COLUMBIA

Launch	**July 16, 1969**
Height	**36 feet (11 m)**
Diameter	**12.8 feet (3.9 m)**
Cabin volume	**220 cubic feet (6.2 cu m)**
Crew	**3**
Organization	**NASA**

WEIGHT ON EARTH

66,000 pounds (30,000 kg)

The Crew

The three members of the crew were men who already had much experience at NASA. They were all part of the Gemini program, a very important preparation for landing on the Moon and walking on its surface. Armstrong and Aldrin were the first human beings to set foot on the Moon. Collins orbited around the Moon at an altitude of 69 miles (111 km).

Neil Armstrong
(b. 1930)
carried out his first mission on board Gemini 8 in 1966. He was the first person to set foot on the Moon. He retired from NASA in 1971.

Michael Collins
(b. 1930)
was the third astronaut to carry out a space walk with the Gemini 10 mission. He was the command module pilot of the Columbia.

Edwin Aldrin
(b. 1930)
took part in the Gemini 13 training mission and was the second man to set foot on lunar soil.

The Moon Without Secrets

Six Apollo missions were able to land on the lunar surface. Apollo 13, because of an oxygen-tank explosion, flew to the Moon but did not make a landing. Through the intelligence and expertise of the astronauts onboard, it was able to return to Earth safely. With the success of these missions, the Moon was no longer unreachable. A dozen men were able to walk on the gray, crunchy lava soil strewn with craters. Each one of these voyages, besides bringing back data, encouraged the development of space science and increased the desire to carry out other missions to different locations of the solar system. ●

The Apollo Missions

The Apollo program began in July 1960. An important modern technological triumph, it succeeded in putting the United States ahead in the space race. Six missions made landings: Apollo 11, 12, 14, 15, 16, and 17. The Apollo lunar module was the first spacecraft designed to fly in a vacuum without any aerodynamic capabilities.

THE LUNAR ROVER

An electric vehicle used by the astronauts to explore the surface of the Moon

High-gain Antenna

Low-gain Antenna

Television Camera

Manual Controls

Television Camera

Lunar Communications Transmission Unit

Storage Locker

Data Console

TWENTY-ONE CHOSEN
Apollo included seven missions designed to land on the Moon, with a total of 21 astronauts. Six missions completed landings, and 12 astronauts walked on the Moon's surface.

740 pounds
(336 kg)

LUNAR MATERIAL
The samples of lunar rocks turned out to be similar to those in the Earth's mantle.

15.5 miles
(25 km)

DISTANCE TRAVELED
The total distance traveled by the Lunar Rover in the Apollo 15, 16, and 17 missions

301:51'50"

STAY
The duration of the Apollo 17 mission, the longest, was almost 302 hours.

HAPPY ENDING
The Apollo-Soyuz mission ended the space race to the Moon.

APOLLO MISSIONS

1970
APOLLO 13
The explosion of the liquid-oxygen tank of the service module forced an early return of the crew: James Lovell, Fred Haise, and John Swigert.

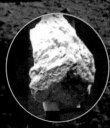

1972
SAMPLES
During the last lunar Apollo mission, the Apollo 17, the astronauts Eugene Cernan and Harrison Schmitt drove over the Moon in the Lunar Rover and took rock samples from the surface.

1975
APOLLO-SOYUZ
The spacecraft Apollo and the Soviet Soyuz docked in space in the first and historic joint mission between NASA and the Soviet Space Agency. It was the last Apollo mission.

The Lunar Orbiter

The Lunar Prospector was launched in 1998 and was in space for 19 months. It orbited the Moon at an altitude of miles (100 km), traveling at a velocity of 400 mph (5,500 km/h), completing an orbit every two hours. This allowed it to obtain data om the surface. Its objective was to attain a w polar orbit of the Moon, which included a apping of the surface, reconnaissance for the mposition and possible deposits of water the form of ice, and measuring the lunar agnetic and gravitational fields.

LUNAR POLE
Images taken by the Lunar Prospector

LUNAR PROSPECTOR

consists of a cylinder covered with thousands of photovoltaic panels.

Solar Sensors

Antenna used to maintain communications with the Earth.

Gamma-Ray Spectrometer searches for potassium, oxygen, uranium, aluminum, silicon, calcium, magnesium, and titanium.

Thrusters

Magnetometer looks for magnetic fields near the spacecraft.

Solar Panel

Alpha Particle Spectrometer detects particles emitted by radioactive gases.

Neutron Spectrometer detects neutrons on the lunar surface.

LUNAR PROSPECTOR

Launch	**January 1998**
Flight to the Moon	**105 hours**
Weight	**650 pounds (295 kg)**
Cost	**$63 million**
Organization	**NASA**

ANTENNAS permit communication with NASA's Deep Space Network.

Sample Collection Bag

LUNAR ROVER

Launch	**July 1971**
Length	**10.2 feet (3.10 m)**
Width	**3.7 feet (1.14 m)**
Velocity	**10 mph (16 km/h)**
Organization	**NASA**

ANTENNA High-gain, in the form of an umbrella on the Lunar Rover

WEIGHT ON EARTH

406 pounds
(209 kg)

WEIGHT ON THE MOON

77 pounds
(35 kg)

End of the Apollo Program

After six landings on the Moon, the Apollo program was terminated. Apollo 18, 19, and 20 were canceled for budgetary reasons. The program had put the United States in the lead of the space race.

APOLLO 13
The pilot of the unfortunate Apollo 13 mission, which was aborted because of an explosion on board the service module

James A. Lovell, Jr.
(b. 1928)
was the backup commander for the Gemini 4 flight and command pilot of Gemini 7 and 12.

SCIENTIST
The only civilian on the Moon. He traveled on board Apollo 17 and was the first geologist to work on the Moon.

Harrison Schmitt
(b. 1928)
North American geologist who flew on the last Apollo mission

APOLLO-SOYUZ
Russian cosmonaut Leonov was part of the Apollo-Soyuz test project in which the two craft remained docked for seven days.

Aleksey Leonov
(b. 1934)
was born in Siberia. During the Voshkod 2 mission, he was the first person to walk in space.

ATER MISSIONS

1994 CLEMENTINE
The spacecraft Clementine orbited the Moon and mapped its surface. It was also used to obtain radar data on the unlit craters near the Moon's south pole.

2003 SMART
The ESA launched Smart 1, its first unmanned spacecraft, with the Moon as its destination. Its purpose was to analyze unexplored regions and to test new technologies, such as solar ionic propulsion.

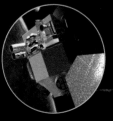

2009 LRO
NASA launched a rocket carrying the Lunar Reconnaissance Orbiter to the south pole of the Moon to look for water that could be used on future missions.

Echoes of the Past

Thanks to the data obtained in 2001 from NASA's WMAP (Wilkinson Microwave Anisotropy Probe), scientists have succeeded in making the first detailed map of cosmic background radiation, a remnant of the big bang. The conclusion of the experts is that this map reveals clues about when the first generation of stars was formed. ●

OMNIDIRECTIONAL ANTENNA

WMAP

Launch	June 30, 2001
Useful life	27 months (3 months for travel and 24 for observation)
Deactivated	2010
Organization	NASA

DIMENSIONS

12.
(3

16.4 feet
(5 m)

ITS PARTS

PROFILE VIEW

PRIMARY REFLECTORS provide the desired angular resolution; can point in any direction.

Line of Sig

PASSIVE THERMAL RADIATOR

INCOMING IMAGES

THERMALLY INSULATED CYLINDRICAL INSTRUMENT

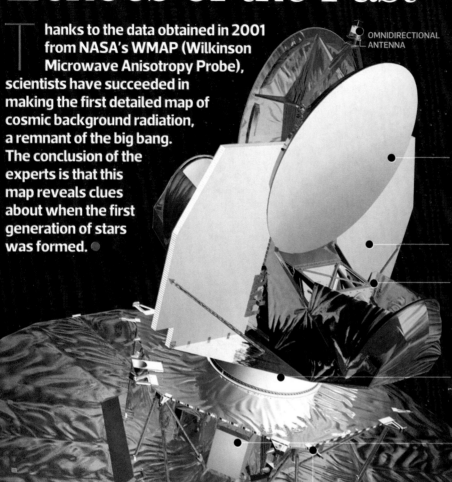

WARM SECTION
Contains:
-Electronic instrumentation
-Position and propulsion control
-Managing information and comma
-Battery and power control

STAR TRACKER

PROTECTIVE SHIELD TO PROVIDE THE SPACECRAFT WITH SHADE

419
watts
OF POWER

1,850 pounds
(840 kg)

WEIGHT ON EARTH

1973
SKYLAB
The launching of the first American space station, Skylab

1976
VIKING
American satellite, takes photos of the surface of Mars

1977
VOYAGER 1 AND 2
Fly by Jupiter in 1979 and Saturn in 1980.

1981
SPACE SHUTTLE
The first manned mission was conducted with the shuttle *Columbia*.

1986
MIR
The first phase of the Russian space station Mir was successfully put into orbit.

1989
COBE
First results concernin the cosmology of the universe.

Observation

Before it was decommissioned in 2010, the WMAP observed the heavens from a point called Lagrange L2, which is 900,000 miles (1.5 million km) from the Earth. This point provides a stable orbit far from the influence of the Earth. Sun shields protected its instruments, which always pointed away from the Sun. WMAP observed the universe in several stages and measured temperature differences between various regions of the cosmos. Every six months it completely covered the entire sky, which made it possible to compare different maps to check data consistency.

Day 90 (3 months)

The probe completed coverage of one half of the sky by day 90. Each hour it covered a sector of 22.5°.

Axial rotation
129 seconds

Precession of the equinoxes: 22.5° around the Sol-WMAP line.

WMAP TRAJECTORY

Before heading for point L2, the probe made a flyby of the Moon to get a gravity boost toward L2.

PLAN VIEW

Lunar Orbit

Orbital Phases

Earth

SUN

L2

WMAP

Encounter with the Moon

900,000 MILES
(1.5 MILLION KM)

Day 180 (6 months)

The whole sky had been mapped by day 180. This was repeated many more times.

The purpose of observing the entire sky every six months was to obtain redundancy in the data gathered over nine years. The maps were compared to test their consistency.

Sun

Earth

WMAP

Terrestrial Orbit

Day 1

Because WMAP had the ability to focus on the sky in two directions simultaneously, it was capable of observing a large portion of the sky every day.

Every 24 hours, WMAP observed 30 percent of the sky.

THE MAP

The various colors of the regions in the detailed map of the sky correspond to very slight differences in temperature in cosmic background radiation. This radiation, the remains of the big bang, was discovered in the 1960s, but only recently has it been possible to describe it in detail.

POLARIZED ZONES

In a photograph of March 31, 2006, polarized zones are visible in different areas of the universe.

Temperature difference between two points, measured by WMAP

Regions of greater-than-average temperatures

COBE, the Predecessor

The results obtained by COBE in 1989 set the stage for the future. The resolution is lower, so much less detail is visible.

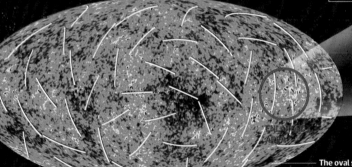

ENLARGED AREA

Regions of below-average temperatures

The oval shape is a projection to show the entire sky.

1990
HUBBLE
One of the most powerful telescopes was put into orbit.

1997
PATHFINDER
The probe released a robot that took photographs on the surface of Mars.

1998
ISS
The first module of the International Space Station is launched.

2001
WMAP
WMAP is launched to obtain the most precise data about the universe.

2004
SPIRIT
The robot, together with its twin Opportunity, reached the surface of Mars.

2005
MRO
Launched in 2005, the probe found traces of water on Mars.

Flying Through Space

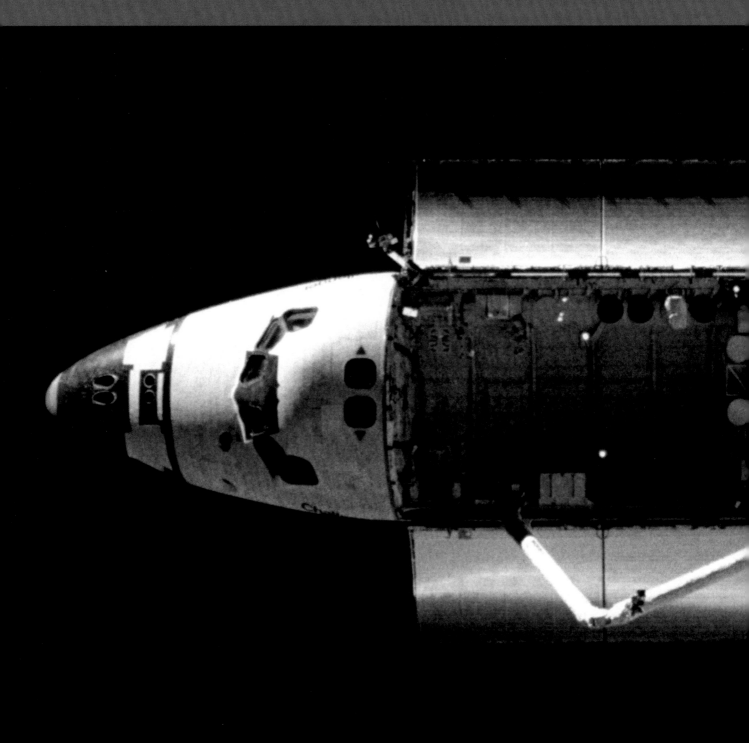

With space vehicles that have ever more capabilities, humans have attained many goals in space, such as making new discoveries about the origin and structure of the other planets. Beginning in 1981 the space shuttle became a key component in astronautics. Life onboard the shuttle is still difficult, and there are still many problems to be solved. However, the future of the human species over the long term is in space, and there is no choice but to follow that path. Like our ancestors, who immigrated to new regions of the planet to survive and prosper, we have a destiny that will take us away from the Earth to find new places to live. ●

Defying Gravity

The human body is suited for conditions under Earth's gravity. Therefore, if the force of gravity increases or decreases, the body feels a distinct, unfamiliar sensation. It causes a decrease in heartbeat; muscles become weaker and bones lose calcium. Engineers and medical doctors have investigated how humans can survive long periods where there is little gravity without causing the body to atrophy. Orbiting laboratories have been built to experiment with zero gravity on Earth. ●

Microgravity

Gravitation is the universal force of attraction between two bodies. It depends on two principal factors: mass and distance. The greater the mass, the greater will be the attraction; on the other hand, with greater distance, the force of gravity is less. A spacecraft in orbit is essentially constantly falling around the Earth, and astronauts aboard do not feel the force of gravity even though they are being pulled by the Earth's gravity. This condition of seeming weightlessness is called a microgravity environment.

ACTION AND REACTION
Newton's third law says that when one body exerts a force on another, the second one exercises an equal force on the first in the opposite direction.

REACTION
44 pounds (20 kg)

ACTION
44 pounds (20 kg)

LEGS
During weightlessness, an astronaut's legs get thinner from lack of exercise, and the muscles atrophy.

arabolic Flight

To achieve microgravity, a C–135 aircraft ascends at an angle of 47° until the pilot shuts off the engines and the plane begins free fall by following a parabolic trajectory. ring this phase, everything in the airplane floats, th equipment and people, because they are in a eightless condition. Such flights are organized by SA, ESA, and RSA (the Russian Space Agency).

LIQUIDS
disperse in the air during conditions of microgravity.

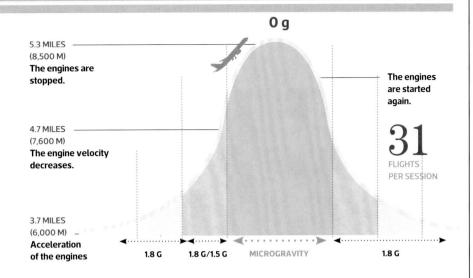

0 g

5.3 MILES
(8,500 M)
The engines are stopped.

The engines are started again.

4.7 MILES
(7,600 M)
The engine velocity decreases.

31
FLIGHTS
PER SESSION

3.7 MILES
(6,000 M)
Acceleration of the engines

1.8 G   1.8 G/1.5 G   MICROGRAVITY   1.8 G

WITHIN THE AIRPLANE
During parabolic flights, nine to 15 scientific experiments can be performed.

15
EXPERIMENTS
PERFORMED

EXPERIMENT 8
Studying smell and taste

EXPERIMENT 7
Testing a new shower system for the astronauts

EXPERIMENT 15
The behavior of ferro-fluids

FREE-FLIGHT ZONE

WEIGHTLESSNESS
A body floats in space.

Water: Another Method for Simulating Weight Reduction

Other methods of training for the astronauts make use of a gigantic swimming pool in which an environment can be created to simulate working in microgravity. In the Johnson Space Center a simulator was installed, completely underwater, which allowed the mission crew that was to be sent to repair the Hubble telescope to test what the working conditions inside the space shuttle would be.

RAVITATIONAL
SISTANCE
me spacecraft take vantage of the gravitational rce of the planets so that ey can increase their speed get to their destination. This the case with the spacecraft ssini, among others.

Sun

Venus

Earth

— TRAJECTORY OF THE CASSINI SPACECRAFT

Saturn

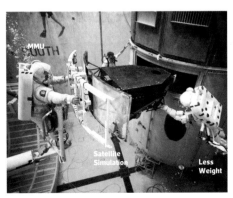

MMU

Satellite Simulation

Less Weight

Point of Departure

Spacecraft launching sites typically meet one or more optimal criteria. For example, choosing a location close to the Equator makes it easier to put a spacecraft into orbit. Moreover, a number of coastal areas have been chosen, because they are more accessible for the transport of the goods needed to build the launch vehicles. The danger of an accident during launch must also be taken into account. Therefore, sites have been chosen in areas with low-density population, such as Cape Canaveral, Florida. ●

Vehicle Assembly Building

The spaceport has an immense building for the preparation and assembly of rockets and of the external shuttle tank. The dimensions of the building are impressive: 525 feet (160 m) high and 518 feet (158 m) wide. The orbiter travels on top of the crawler-transporter from this building to the launch pad.

ASSEMBLY BUILDING

CRAWLER-TRANSPORTER

LAUNCHER PLATFORM

ROTATING SERVICE STRUCTURE has a height of 189 feet (57.6 m) and moves in a semicircular path around the shuttle.

Fixed Service Structure

This steel giant is located at the launch pad. It consists of fixed and rotating structures. Atop the transport caterpillar, the mobile launch platform brings the space shuttle to this location.

ROTATING SERVICE STRUCTURE protects the shuttle while the contamination-free fuels are being pumped into the tanks.

ELEVATOR When the astronauts arrive at the launch pad, they ride the elevator to a facility called the white room. From there, they enter the shuttle.

LIGHTNING RODS

The mast protects people, the shuttle, and the other platform components from lightning. It is located in the upper part of the fixed structure and is 348 feet (106 m) tall.

FIXED SERVICE STRUCTURE

The structure is 246 feet (75 m) high and divided into 12 floors. It has three arms that connect it to the shuttle.

ORBITER ACCESS ARM

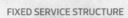

Floating Platform

Earth–based launching platforms are very expensive. For this reason, some countries have developed floating launch platforms. At sea it is much simpler and safer to pick a location at the Equator, where the Earth's rotational velocity is the greatest, an advantage for putting space missions into orbit.

SPACE ROCKET

PLATFORM

1 **MOUNTING**
A rocket is built on an assembly barge 660 feet (200 m) long.

2 **TRANSFER**
The rocket is transferred to the launching platform Odyssey.

3 **STORAGE**
The rocket is stored until launch. The assembly barge leaves the location.

PROPULSION ROCKETS

WHITE ROOM
Exclusively for astronauts. From here they go to the shuttle.

OTHER LAUNCHING BASES

The preference to use locations close to the Equator for spaceports has an explanation. The speed of rotation of the Earth's surface is greatest at the Equator, and vehicles launched near the Equator can take advantage of that speed to help reach orbit.

FIRST LAUNCHES FROM THE MOST IMPORTANT BASES

PLESETSK (1966)

KENNEDY (1967)

EQUATOR

KOUROU (1970)

SAN MARCO (1967)

USA

NASA
Endeavour

TAIL SERVICE MAST

These structures connect the platform with the spacecraft. They provide oxygen and hydrogen to the external tanks.

130 ft (40 m)

CRAWLER-TRANSPORTER

The orbiter sits on top of two caterpillar tracks and is carried to the launch pad. A system of laser rays precisely guide it as it moves at 2 mph (3.2 km/h).

The Rockets

eveloped in the first half of the 20th century, rockets are necessary for sending any kind of object into space. They produce sufficient force to leave the ground together with their cargo and in a short time acquire the velocity necessary to reach orbit in space around the Earth. On average, more than one rocket per week is sent into space from somewhere in the world.

COMPONENTS

Payload System

Guidance System

Propulsion System

ACCORDING TO THE FUEL TYPE THEY USE, THESE WOULD BE CONSIDERED CHEMICAL (FUEL) ROCKETS.

In liquid-fuel rockets, hydrogen and oxygen are in separate containers. In solid-fuel rockets, they are mixed and contained in a single cylinder.

KEY
Gases expelled

LIQUID   SOLID   HYBRID

Engine Operation

Before liftoff, the fuel is ignited. The boosters ignite only if the ignition of the main engine is successful. The rocket lifts off, and two minutes later the boosters are extinguished, their fuel completely consumed. The main engine remains attached until its fuel is used up, and it is then jettisoned.

ARIANE 5

First operational flight	Oct. 11, 1999
Diameter	16 feet (5 m)
Total height	167 feet (51 m)
Booster rocket weight	610,000 pounds (277,000 kg) each (full)
Geosynchronous payload	15,000 pounds (6,800 kg)
Organization	ESA

Boeing   Space Shuttle   Ariane 5

1,645,000 pounds
(746,000 kg)

WEIGHT OF ARIANE 5

THERMAL INSULATION
To protect the combustion chamber from high temperatures of the burning fuel, the walls are sprayed with rocket fuel. This process manages to cool the engine off.

CONICAL NOSE CONE protects the cargo.

UPPER PAYLOAD Up to two satellites

LOWER PAYLOAD Up to two satellites

LIQUID OXYGEN TANK contains 286,000 pounds (130,000 kg) for combustion.

UPPER ENGINES release the satellite at a precise angle and speed.

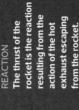

STRUCTURE OF THE
MAIN ENGINE

LIQUID
HYDROGEN TANK

LIQUID
OXYGEN TANK

FUEL PUMP

COMBUSTION
CHAMBER

COVER   PROPELLANT   INSULATION

TYPE OF ROCKET DEPENDING ON ITS PROPULSION

Rockets with chemical propellants are the most common. Their thrust comes from the exhaust produced through combustion. For propulsion in space, an ion drive can be used to produce an exhaust of accelerated ions (electrically charged atoms). The use of nuclear energy has been studied as a possible source of energy for heating a gas to produce an exhaust.

KEY

Thrust

WATER
OR LIQUID HYDROGEN

FUEL

IONS

NUCLEAR
REACTOR

CHEMICAL

NUCLEAR

IONIC

LIQUID
HYDROGEN
TANK
contains
225 tons.

COHETE
AUXILIAR

esa

cnes

CONNECTOR
TUBE

How It Works

To do its job, the rocket must overcome gravity. As it rises, the mass of the rocket is reduced through the burning of its fuel. Moreover, because the distance from the Earth increases, the effect of gravity decreases.

ACTION AND
REACTION

The thrust of the rocket is the reaction resulting from the action of the hot exhaust escaping from the rocket.

BOOSTER
ROCKETS
burn fuel for two minutes.

THRUSTERS
expel gases so that the rocket can begin its ascent.

LIQUID
HELIUM

MAIN
ENGINE
burns for 10 minutes.

ROCKET
THRUST

EARTH GRAVITY

1926
On March 16, Robert Hutchings Goddard launched the first liquid-fueled rocket in the United States.

1942
V2 rockets were being built by the Germans for military use. They were the first rockets to be built on a large scale.

1961
The Soviet rocket Vostok 1 lifts the first astronaut, Yury Gagarin, into space; he orbits the Earth at an altitude of 196 miles (315 km).

1969
The rocket Saturn V sends a man to the Moon on the Apollo 11 mission. The giant rocket is more than 330 feet (100 m) high.

1988
The powerful rocket Energia puts a prototype Soviet space shuttle, the Buran, into orbit.

1999
After two failed attempts in 1996 and 1998, the Ariane 5 achieves its first successful commercial flight.

Launch Sequence

S carcely 50 years have elapsed since the first spaceflights. Nevertheless, access to space—whether for placing satellites into orbit, sending probes to other planets, or launching astronauts into space—has become almost routine and is a good business for countries that have launch capabilities. Preparations for launch begin with the assembly of the rocket, followed by its placement on a launch pad. When its engines are ignited, the rocket rises into the atmosphere. Once the atmosphere has been left behind, less thrust is needed. For this reason, rockets consist of two or more stages stacked on top of each other. Booster rockets are typically used to produce greater initial thrust. ●

Bound for Space

HOW IT FLIES

The hot gases produced by the burning fuel push in all directions.

As the gases escape through the open nozzle, they generate an opposing force.

Fuel tank

Gas direction

Nozzle

FLIGHT GUIDANCE

The rocket's guidance computer uses data from laser gyroscopes to control the inclination of the nozzles, directing the rocket along its proper flight path.

Laser Gyroscope

Electrical Signals

Computer

Gimbals

Nozzle Inclination

STAGES

The Ariane 5 has a main stage, an upper stage, and two booster rockets. The main stage and booster rockets are ignited at launch.

The upper stage, which carries the payload, is ignited once it reaches space.

The main stage uses liquid hydrogen and oxygen.

The booster rockets are solid-fuel rockets.

Fairing

The fairing is jettisoned when the air becomes so thin that wind no longer poses any danger to the payload.

Final phase

The work of the upper stage begins. The upper-stage rocket is the only rocket not used on the launching pad. Instead it is used to insert the payload into its proper orbit. The rocket can be reignited after it is shut down and can burn for a total of 19 minutes.

00:10:00

The main stage, ignited at the end of the countdown, separates and falls back to Earth. Its supply of liquid hydrogen and oxygen has been used up.

Launch Window

Direction of the Earth's rotation

Launch Window

Latitude of the launching point

Ideal trajectory

Planned orbit

Projection of the orbit

Rockets must be launched at predetermined times, which depend on the objective of the launch. If the objective is to place a satellite into orbit, the latitude of the launched rocket needs to coincide with the trajectory of the desired orbit. When the mission involves docking with another object in space, the launch window might fall within only a few minutes.

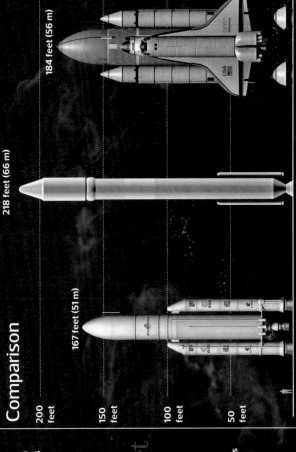

Comparison

218 feet (66 m)

184 feet (56 m)

167 feet (51 m)

200 feet

150 feet

100 feet

50 feet

ARIANE 5

Weight at launch: 822 tons (746 t)

First operational flight: 1999

Maximum payload: 7.5 to 17.6 tons (6.8-16 t) depending on the desired orbit

DELTA IV M+

Weight at launch: 330 tons (300 t)

First operational launch: 2002

Maximum payload: 6 to 12.9 tons (5.5-11.7 t) depending on the desired orbit

SPACE SHUTTLE

Weight at launch: 2,200 tons (2,000 t)

First operational launch: 1981

Maximum payload: 27.5 tons (25 t) into low Earth orbit

The countdown for the Ariane 5 typically lasts six hours. At the end of the countdown, the launch begins with the ignition of the main stage's liquid-fuel engine. Seven seconds later the two solid-fuel boosters are ignited. Before the boosters' ignition, the flight can be aborted by shutting down the main stage.

-06:00:00
The launch countdown begins.

-04:30:00
The tanks begin to be filled.

-01:00:00
Mechanical reinforcements are made.

Detachment

Explosive bolts separate the boosters from the main stage and the main stage from the second stage.

-00:05:30
The automatic launch sequence starts.

00:00:00
The main-stage engines are ignited.

00:00:07
The solid-fuel boosters are ignited. The rocket begins to lift off 0.3 second later.

00:02:10
At 200,000 feet (60,000 m) the solid-fuel boosters separate and fall to the ocean in a secure area.

363 feet (111 m)

The height of the Saturn V, the largest rocket ever launched. It was used in the late 1960s and early 1970s to take astronauts to the Moon. During launching it could be heard 90 miles (150 km) away.

Solid-fuel boosters

provide 90 percent of the initial thrust needed to launch the Ariane 5. The boosters are 102 feet (31 m) high and contain 525,000 pounds (238,000 kg) of fuel. Once the fuel is used up, the boosters are separated from the main stage. 130 seconds into the flight.

Space Shuttle

Before the Space Shuttle program ended in 2011, the US space shuttle served many purposes. In addition to making flights to the International Space Station, these vehicles were also reused to lift satellites into space and put them into low Earth orbit. The US fleet has three shuttles: *Discovery*, *Atlantis*, and *Endeavour*, all of which are now retired. The *Challenger* exploded in 1986 and the *Columbia* in 2003.

SATELLITE remains in the payload bay and is moved by the arm.

TECHNICAL DATA FOR THE SPACE SHUTTLE

First launch	April 12–14, 1981
Mission length	5–20 days
Width	78 feet (23 m)
Length	122 feet (37 m)
Organization	NASA

165,000 pounds
WEIGHT ON EARTH
(74,842 kg)

Boeing Aircraft

Standard Airplane

122 feet (37 m)
Space Shuttle

EXTERNAL FUEL TANK

SPACE ORBITER

AUXILIARY ROCKETS

ROBOT ARM moves satellites in and out of the payload bay.

SPACE ORBITER

The Cabin

The place where the members of the crew live is divided into two levels: an upper level houses the pilot and the copilot (and up to two more astronauts), and a lower level is used for daily living. The amount of habitable space inside the cabin is 2,470 cubic feet (70 cu m).

CONTROLS
There are more than 2,000 separate controls in the flight cabin, three times as many as in Apollo.

COMMAND CONSOLE

PILOT SEAT

CONTROL CABIN

COMMANDER'S CHAIR

COMMAND CABIN

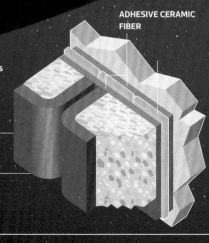

Discovery

ADHESIVE CERAMIC FIBER

CERAMICS make up the layers that protect the spacecraft from heat.

GLASS COVERING

SILICON CERAMIC TILES

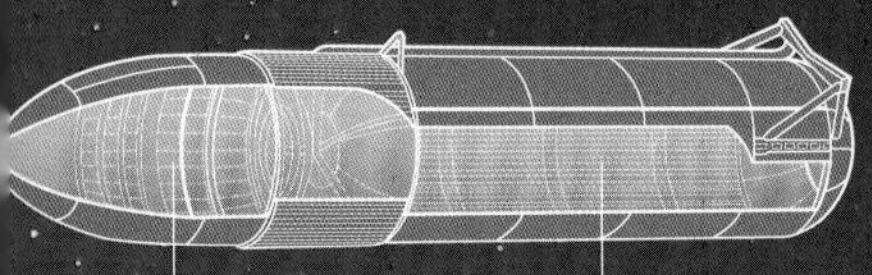

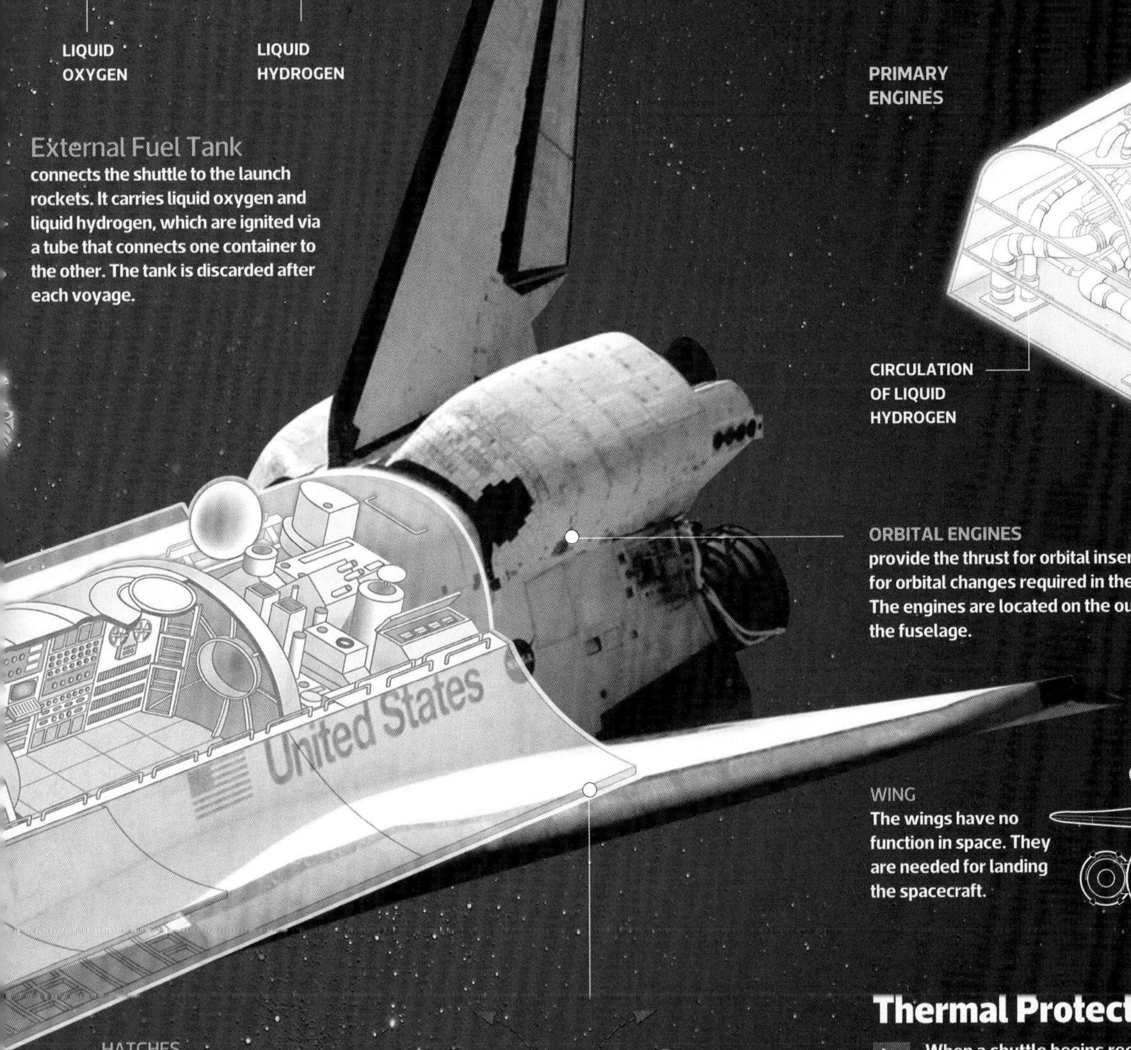

Primary Engines

There are three primary engines, which are fed by oxygen and liquid hydrogen from the external tank. Each engine has computer-based controls that make adjustments to obtain the correct thrust and mix of fuel.

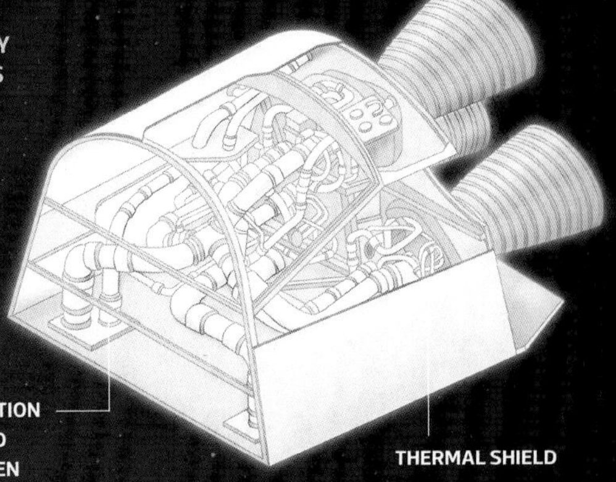

PRIMARY
ENGINES

CIRCULATION
OF LIQUID
HYDROGEN

THERMAL SHIELD

**LIQUID
OXYGEN**

**LIQUID
HYDROGEN**

External Fuel Tank

connects the shuttle to the launch rockets. It carries liquid oxygen and liquid hydrogen, which are ignited via a tube that connects one container to the other. The tank is discarded after each voyage.

ORBITAL ENGINES
provide the thrust for orbital insertion and for orbital changes required in the orbit. The engines are located on the outside of the fuselage.

WING
The wings have no function in space. They are needed for landing the spacecraft.

United States

HATCHES
are opened when the orbiter reaches low Earth orbit. They have thermal panels that protect the spacecraft from overheating.

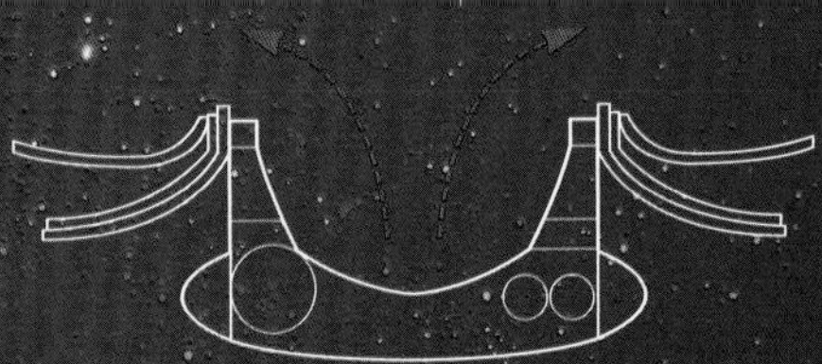

Thermal Protection

When a shuttle begins reentry from Earth's orbit, friction heats the surface to a temperature between 570 and 2,700° F (300–1,500° C). Various parts of the spacecraft must have protective layers to keep them from melting. The inner parts of the wings and the nose heat up the most.

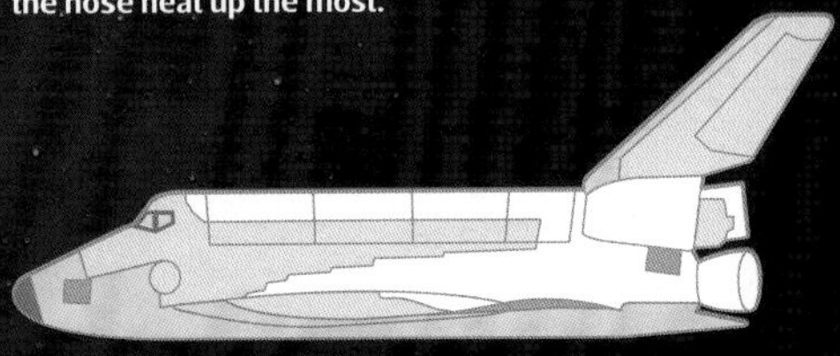

Solid-Fuel Rockets

are designed to last for some 20 flights. After each flight, they are recovered from the ocean and refurbished. They carry the shuttle to an altitude of 27 miles (44 km) and are capable of supporting the entire weight of the shuttle while standing on the ground.

IGNITION
SECTOR

SOLID
FUEL

THRUST
NOZZLE

KEY

Ceramic fiber: temperature below 700° F (370° C)

Silicon ceramic: 700–1,200° F (370–648° C)

1,200–2,300° F (648–1,260° C)-also silicon

Metal or glass, without thermal protection

Carbon in areas above 2,300° F (1,260° C)

ORBITAL SPECIFICATIONS

Orbital altitude	190–330 miles (310–530 km)
Orbital period	97 minutes
Average orbital speed	17,200 mph (27,800 km/h)

Front View

Back View

ORBITAL
MANEUVERING
SYSTEM

00:02:00
27 MILES (44 KM) ALTITUDE:
THE SOLID-FUEL ROCKETS
ARE JETTISONED.

BOOSTER ROCKETS
are jettisoned and begin
to fall toward Earth. Later
they will be refurbished.

ASCENDING PHASE
**The space shuttle turns 120° and ascends
upside down, with the crew in an
upside-down position. It maintains this
position until reaching orbit.**

00:00:00

LIFTOFF
**The two solid-fuel rockets
and the three main engines
go into action. They burn two
million pounds (900,000 kg)
of propellant, and the shuttle
reaches an altitude of 27 miles
(44 km). The solid fuel is
completely consumed.**

COMPARTMENT WITH
THREE PARACHUTES
Used for jettisoning the
rockets

CARGO BAY
carries the apparatus that
will be put into orbit.

2,200 tons
THE LIFTOFF WEIGHT OF THE
SPACE SHUTTLE

BOOSTER ROCKETS
provide the thrust
essential for liftoff.

EXTERNAL
TANK
carries fuel
to be used in
liftoff.

SHUTTLE
houses the astronauts and
the cargo once in orbit.

00:08:00
THE EXTERNAL
TANK IS JETTISONED.

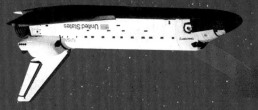

ORBITAL MANEUVERING CONTROL
SYSTEM
**puts the shuttle into an appropriate orbit.
Depending on the mission, its altitude could
be as high as 700 miles (1,100 km).**

2

5-30 DAYS

ORBITS IN SPACE
**Once the necessary altitude has been
reached for the mission, the shuttle remains
in space between 10 and 16 days. It is then
oriented for the return flight to Earth.**

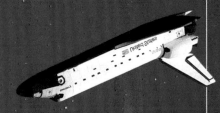

XTERNAL TANK
fuel is fed to the shuttle
ngines until just before the
huttle reaches orbit. The tank
immediately jettisoned and
it falls it burns up through
mospheric friction.

17,400 mph
(28,000 km/h)
SPEED REACHED BY THE SHUTTLE

3

REENTRY INTO THE ATMOSPHERE
**The shuttle undergoes a communications
blackout because of the heated air that
surrounds it.**

Retrieval System
**Two minutes after the shuttle's liftoff, the
booster rockets have burned up their fuel.
They are jettisoned, and the parachutes
eploy for their fall into the ocean. Later the
ooster rockets are retrieved by ships and
furbished.**

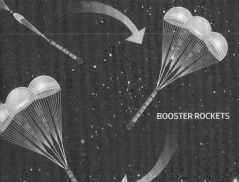

BOOSTER ROCKETS

4

LANDING
**The shuttle landing sequence is
completely automatic and kicks in two
minutes before returning to terra firma. It
lands on a runway 3 miles (5 km) long.**

4,900° F
(1,500° C)
MAXIMUM TEMPERATURE

20°
LANDING ANGLE

TURNS
**It makes various "S"
turns to reduce its
velocity.**

Far from Home

he experience of leaving the Earth to live in a space station or to take a trip in the shuttle is a fascinating adventure. Life in orbit requires many adjustments to survive in an environment where there is no water, air pressure, or oxygen. The crew cabin is pressurized, and water is produced electrically with oxygen and hydrogen. Food requires special packaging, and the garbage is pulverized.

Crew Cabin

The crew cabin is located at the front of the shuttle. The control deck is on the upper level, and the lower level has sleeping and living compartments as well as the hatch for entering and leaving the cabin.

CABIN

DORMITORY

BATHROOM

CUPBOARD

HATCH

Physical Ailments

The human body is accustomed to Earth's gravity. In space the astronauts experience weightlessness, floating in the spacecraft. Life in space can have undesirable effects on the body, such as bone and muscle reduction. In many cases, living in small spaces can cause psychological problems. Also, radiation from solar storms can cause severe damage.

Hallucinations and Seasickness

RESPIRATORY SYSTEM

CIRCULATORY SYSTEM

MUSCULAR SYSTEM

LOSS OF CALCIUM IN THE BONES
In microgravity, the bone tissue is not regenerated but absorbed by other tissues. The loss of mass can appear as an excess of calcium in other parts of the body (for example, kidney stones).

Diseased Bone

Healthy Bone

TETHER
holds down the body to keep it from floating.

1

SLEEP
Once a day
The Sun rises and sets every hour and a half when the shuttle is in orbit, but the astronauts attempt to sleep eight hours once a day. They must stay tethered to keep from floating.

90 minutes
THE LENGTH OF A DAY IN ORBIT

Sleeping Bag

2

TOILET
To go to the bathroom, a system of suction with air is used because it is impossible to use water. Baths can be taken. After a bath, the same clothes are used because there is no way to wash clothes in space.

EARPHONES
help maintain communication.

3

FOOD
Three times a day
Every day the astronauts have breakfast, lunch, and dinner. They must bring the food to their mouths very carefully. They must drink enough water or they could begin to suffer from dehydration.

CLOTHES
Comfortable clothes are used during the day.

4

WORK
Eight hours a day
They work four hours on Saturdays and have Sundays off. Weekdays are normal workdays. The most common tasks are scientific experiments and normal maintenance.

5

EXERCISE
Two hours a day
Every day, in order to stay in good health, astronauts must do physical exercises. Because weightlessness causes muscle loss, exercises that tone the muscles are performed.

Work Clothes in Space

Device to Increase Muscle Tone

72
72 VARIETIES OF DISHES

20
VARIETIES OF DRINKS

Profession: Astronaut

How do you become an astronaut? Before undertaking a mission in space, every candidate must submit to rigorous examinations since the tasks they are to perform are very delicate and risky. They must intensively study mathematics, meteorology, astronomy, and physics and become familiar with computers and navigation in space. They must also train physically to get used to low-gravity conditions in orbit and to be able to carry out repairs.

Manned Maneuvering Unit

The training program is difficult and exhausting. There are daily activities in the flight simulators with specialized computers.

FLIGHT SIMULATOR

COMMANDS

COMPUTER

VISOR

DIGITAL CAMERA

IMAGE CONTROLLER

OXYGEN SUPPLY

LIFE-SUPPORT SYSTEM

LIFE-SUPPORT BACKPACK

ASTRONAUT

COMPUTER
Pocket communication equipment.

OXYGEN
comes in through this part of the space suit.

1965
The astronaut Edward White used this space suit to perform a space walk in the vicinity of the Gemini capsule.

1969
Neil Armstrong used this space suit when he performed his first historic space walk on the surface of the Moon.

1984
Bruce McCandless wore this space suit when he became the first person to carry out a space walk without being tethered to the shuttle.

1994
Space shuttle astronauts demonstrate a suit that is much more modern and reusable.

COOLING LIQUID
serves as thermal protection and protection against meteorites.

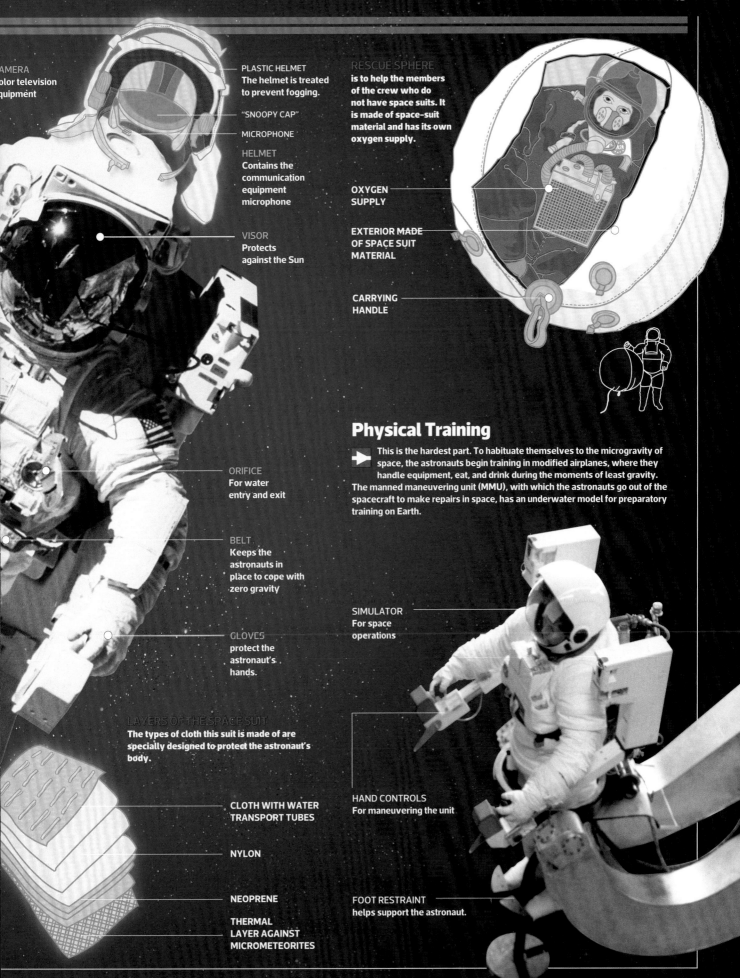

CAMERA
color television
equipment

PLASTIC HELMET
The helmet is treated
to prevent fogging.

"SNOOPY CAP"

MICROPHONE

HELMET
Contains the
communication
equipment
microphone

VISOR
Protects
against the Sun

RESCUE SPHERE
is to help the members
of the crew who do
not have space suits. It
is made of space-suit
material and has its own
oxygen supply.

OXYGEN
SUPPLY

EXTERIOR MADE
OF SPACE SUIT
MATERIAL

CARRYING
HANDLE

ORIFICE
For water
entry and exit

BELT
Keeps the
astronauts in
place to cope with
zero gravity

GLOVES
protect the
astronaut's
hands.

Physical Training

This is the hardest part. To habituate themselves to the microgravity of
space, the astronauts begin training in modified airplanes, where they
handle equipment, eat, and drink during the moments of least gravity.
The manned maneuvering unit (MMU), with which the astronauts go out of the
spacecraft to make repairs in space, has an underwater model for preparatory
training on Earth.

SIMULATOR
For space
operations

LAYERS OF THE SPACE SUIT
The types of cloth this suit is made of are
specially designed to protect the astronaut's
body.

CLOTH WITH WATER
TRANSPORT TUBES

NYLON

NEOPRENE

THERMAL
LAYER AGAINST
MICROMETEORITES

HAND CONTROLS
For maneuvering the unit

FOOT RESTRAINT
helps support the astronaut.

Control from Earth ⚠

onitoring the astronauts' activity is done from operations centers. In the United States, NASA is in charge of the manned missions from the Mission Control Center located in the Johnson Space Center in Houston. The unmanned missions are supervised from the Jet Propulsion Laboratory in Los Angeles. Utilizing telemetry technology, which makes it possible to see technical aspects in real time, the flight controllers carry out their tasks in front of consoles equipped with computers. ●

Houston Space Center Floor Plan

➡ The center was used for the first time in 1964 for the Gemini 4 mission. The operations control room has an auditorium, a screen that projects the locations of tracking stations on the Earth, and another screen showing the passage of satellites in orbit. Computers control all the components of the spacecraft.

SCREEN 1 records the location of the satellites and other objects in orbit.

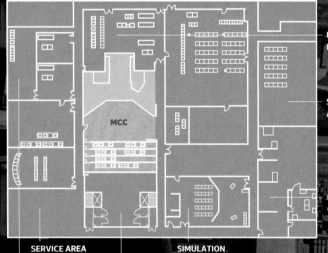

MCC

EXHIBITION ROOM

SERVICE AREA

METEOROLOGICAL CENTER

SERVICE AREA

SUPPORT ROOMS

VISUALIZATION ROOM

SIMULATION ROOM

FLIGHT DIRECTOR

ROW 3 FLIGHT DIRECTION The countdown before liftoff is performed and the flight plan made.

ROW 4 DIRECTORATE The lead authorities are located in the fourth row, from where they coordinate the crew's flight operations.

Console

➡ The Operations Control Room consists of about a hundred consoles. The consoles form desks with an area for more than one monitor. They have drawers and counters for providing a working area.

SPACE MAINTENANCE IS CARRIED OUT

365

DAYS A YEAR

FOLDING TABLE For supporting objects and books

MONITOR To display data from spacecraft and other systems

PROTECTIVE COVERING prevents damage to the console system.

REAR SLIDING DRAWER To keep information and papers

The Big Screen

An enormous screen dominates the Operations Control Center. It gives information on the location and orbital trajectory of a spacecraft in flight as well as other data. The screen is of vital importance for the operators, because it allows for a rapid reading of information to take action efficiently and to prevent accidents.

SCREEN 2
shows the location and path of spacecraft in orbit.

24-*hour days*

TIME THAT THE CENTER IS OPERATING DURING MISSIONS

ROW 1
LIFTOFF MONITOR
Also controls the trajectory and carries out course adjustments of the spacecraft.

ROW 2
MEDICAL SECTION
The second row checks the astronauts' health and establishes communication with the crew.

OPS PLANNER

CAPCOM

CONTROL ROOM
With a gigantic screen to monitor flights

VISITOR'S ROOM
contains seventy-four seats, and it is located at the back of the room.

Space Shuttle Control Center

It is smaller than the Houston Center. About 12 air controllers work there every day, a number that may rise to 20 when a flight is ongoing. Each worker has a different job, with the first row being the lowest in the management hierarchy and the fourth the highest.

1
SPACECRAFT COMMUNICATOR
maintains contact with the astronauts.

2
FLIGHT SURGEON
checks the medical condition of the crew.

3
FLIGHT DIRECTOR
helps the director of mission control.

4
MISSION DIRECTOR
has the main responsibility for flight control.

Permanent Exploration

Space exploration brings scientific ideas to everyone's attention. This is beneficial because it stimulates our creativity and curiosity.

Moreover, these flights contribute to the training of a new generation of scientists. Mars has often been seen as a goal for space exploration, perhaps because of its proximity to Earth and its

THE SPIRIT
Shown with its panels extended, Spirit is one of the robot explorers for studying Martian soil.

relatively hospitable surface. Among the probes that NASA has sent to Mars are two robots, Spirit and Opportunity, that scratched the surface of the Red Planet and sent back very interesting data—they found geologic evidence of ancient environmental conditions in which there was water and in which life could have been present. ●

Satellite Orbits

The space available for placing communications satellites is not unlimited. On the contrary, it is a finite space that could become saturated with too many satellites. Desirable locations in geostationary orbits are already reaching this situation, chock-full of television and other communications satellites. The placement of these instruments cannot be arbitrary; errors of 1 or 2 degrees in position can generate interference with neighboring satellites. The positions are regulated by the International Telecommunications Union. Geostationary satellites have the advantage of being in a fixed position with respect to the Earth's surface. In contrast, satellites in low or medium orbit require a sequence of terrestrial stations to maintain a communications link. •

Different Types

The quality of the information transmitted by the satellites depends on their position relative to the Earth. The geostationary orbit (GEO), which is the most commonly used orbit today, makes it possible to provide coverage to the entire planet with only four satellites, whereas lower orbits need constellations of satellites to get total coverage. This is the case for satellites in LEO (low Earth orbit). In other cases, satellites in MEO (medium Earth orbit) typically describe elliptical orbits. A GEO satellite is in a circular orbit, and if it orbits over the Equator, it always maintains the same position with respect to the Earth.

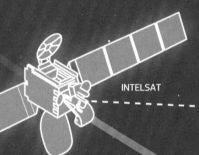

INTELSAT

LEO ORBIT

A low Earth orbit is between 125 and 1,900 miles (200–3,000 km) above the Earth. LEO has been used for telephone communications satellites because of GEO saturation. The orbits are circular and require less transmission power than other orbits. However, they require Earth-based centers to track the satellites.

22,400 miles (36,000 km)

GEO ORBIT

The geostationary orbit (GEO) is the most common, particularly for television satellites. A satellite in a geostationary orbit orbits the Earth in 23 hours and 56 minutes. Because this equals the rotation of the Earth, the satellite remains stationary relative to the Earth's surface. A satellite in GEO orbits 22,400 miles (36,000 km) above the Earth.

EQUATORIAL ORBIT

POLAR ORBIT

ELLIPTIC ORBIT

APOGEE
The point farthest
from the Earth

PERIGEE
The point closest to
the Earth

CIRCULAR ORBIT

The same distance

ORBITS	LEO	MEO	GEO
Distance from the Earth	125–1,900 miles (200–3,000 km)	1,900–22,400 miles (3,000–36,000 km)	22,400 miles (36,000 km)
Satellite cost	Low	Medium	High
Type of network	Complex	Moderate	Simple
Satellite life	3–7 years	10–15 years	10–15 years
Coverage	Short	Medium	Continuous

Frequency Bands

The satellites transmit information in different frequencies depending on their function.

K BAND
Used for instruments in space and for local multipoint transmission. The frequency range lies between 18 and 30 GHz. This band has the greatest capacity for data transmission.

L BAND
Used for the GPS system, cell phones, and digital radio. Operates in frequencies between 1.5 and 2.7 GHz. This band has the least data-transmission capacity.

K BAND
Used for television and radio transmissions. Transmits in a range between 12 and 18 GHz.

LEO ORBIT
MEO ORBIT
GEO ORBIT

GPS

ORBITAL INCLINATION 55°

SPOT

393 miles (2 km)

MEO ORBIT

The altitude of satellites in a medium Earth orbit (MEO) ranges from 20,500 miles (33,000 km) up to the altitude of the geostationary satellites. They generally describe an elliptical orbit. Because putting them in orbit requires more energy than for a satellite in LEO, their cost is greater.

ORBITAL INCLINATION 64.8°

GLONASS

EARTH'S AXIS 23°

11,800 miles (19,000 km)

IRIDIUM

GALILEO

HUBBLE TELESCOPE

ORBITAL INCLINATION 60°

A

INNER VAN ALLEN BELT
Its greatest concentration is about 1,860 miles (3,000 km) above the surface of the Earth.

B

OUTER VAN ALLEN BELT
Primarily between 9,300 and 12,400 miles (15,000 and 20,000 km) above the surface of the Earth

22,400 miles (36,000 km)

is the altitude necessary for the orbit of a satellite so that it will remain stationary with respect to the Earth's surface.

VAN ALLEN BELTS

Regions of the Earth's magnetosphere where charged particles are concentrated and protons and electrons move in spirals. There are two zones of concentrated particles, the inner and outer radiation belts.

Cutting-Edge Technology

n July 1999, the X-ray observatory known as Chandra was put into orbit. Since then, it has provided important information about the universe and its phenomena. Chandra can make X-ray observations of the heavens with an angular resolution of 0.5 seconds of an arc, 1,000 times greater than the first orbital X-ray telescope, the Einstein Observatory. This characteristic permits it to detect sources of light that are 20 times more diffuse. The group in charge of constructing the X-ray telescope had to develop technologies for processes that had never been used before.

Data Transmission

The satellite system provides the structure and the equipment necessary for the telescope and the scientific instruments to operate. A propulsion system gradually puts the spacecraft into its final orbit, which is elliptical and extends far from Earth. In order to control the critical temperature of its components, Chandra has a special system of radiators and thermostats. The temperature near the X-ray mirrors has to be maintained at the proper temperature to keep the mirrors in focus. The electrical energy of the satellite comes from solar panels and is stored in three batteries.

HOW IMAGES ARE CREATED

The information compiled by Chandra is transferred to tables and images with coordinates of the x- and y-axes.

1 TABLE
contains the time, position, and the energy collected by Chandra during its observations.

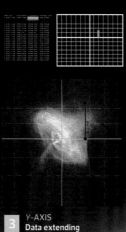

2 X-AXIS
Data extending horizontally on the grid

3 Y-AXIS
Data extending vertically on the grid

TELESCOPE PORT

1. OBSERVATION
The telescopic camera takes X-ray images and sends them to the Deep Space Network for processing.

PHOTOGRAPHIC CAMERA

HIGH-RESOLUTION MIRROR

SOLAR PANEL

X-Rays

Four Hierarchic Hyperboloids

4. CHANDRA X-RAY CONTROL CENTER
It is responsible for operating the observatory and receiving the images. The operators are responsible for preparing commands, determining the altitude, and monitoring the condition and the safety of the satellite.

3. JET PROPULSION LABORATORY
receives information from the Deep Space Network and processes it.

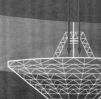

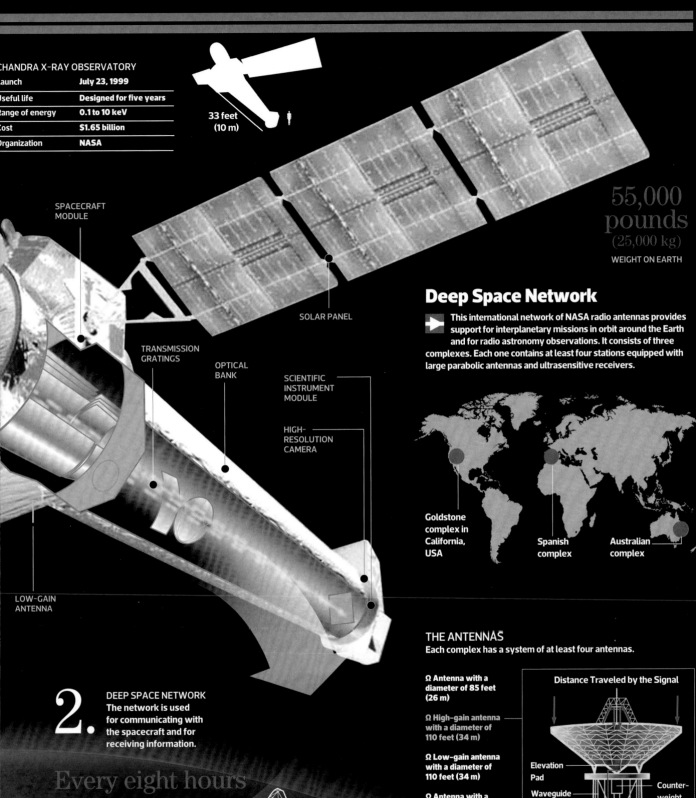

CHANDRA X-RAY OBSERVATORY

Launch	**July 23, 1999**
Useful life	**Designed for five years**
Range of energy	**0.1 to 10 keV**
Cost	**$1.65 billion**
Organization	**NASA**

33 feet
(10 m)

SPACECRAFT
MODULE

55,000
pounds
(25,000 kg)
WEIGHT ON EARTH

SOLAR PANEL

Deep Space Network

This international network of NASA radio antennas provides support for interplanetary missions in orbit around the Earth and for radio astronomy observations. It consists of three complexes. Each one contains at least four stations equipped with large parabolic antennas and ultrasensitive receivers.

TRANSMISSION
GRATINGS

OPTICAL
BANK

SCIENTIFIC
INSTRUMENT
MODULE

HIGH-
RESOLUTION
CAMERA

Goldstone
complex in
California,
USA

Spanish
complex

Australian
complex

LOW-GAIN
ANTENNA

THE ANTENNAS
Each complex has a system of at least four antennas.

Ω Antenna with a
diameter of 85 feet
(26 m)

Ω High-gain antenna
with a diameter of
110 feet (34 m)

Ω Low-gain antenna
with a diameter of
110 feet (34 m)

Ω Antenna with a
diameter of 230 feet
(70 m)

Distance Traveled by the Signal

Elevation
Pad

Waveguide

Counter-
weight

Electronic
Equipment

Mirror

BELOW GROUND

2.

DEEP SPACE NETWORK
The network is used
for communicating with
the spacecraft and for
receiving information.

Every eight hours
Chandra contacts the Deep Space Network.

FIVE YEARS
WAS TO BE THE LIFETIME OF THE
MISSION, BUT IT WAS SURPASSED.

Space Probes

From the first spacecraft, such as Mariner of the mid-1960s, to the Mars Reconnaissance Orbiter launched in 2005 for a close-up study of Mars, space probes have made major contributions. Most of them have been solar-powered; they are the size of an automobile, and they travel to predetermined locations using rockets for thrust. These unmanned machines are equipped with cameras, sensors, spectrometers, and other sophisticated instruments that allow them to study the planets, moons, comets, and asteroids in detail.

APPROACHING MARS

C FINAL ORBIT
The craft attains an almost circular orbit, which is the best-suited for obtaining data.

Orbit

B BRAKING
To reduce the size of its orbit, the spacecraft makes use of atmospheric braking over the next six months.

Number of orbits: 500.

Mars

A INITIAL ORBIT
The first orbit described by the probe was an enormous ellips
Duration: 35 hours.

Mars Reconnaissance Orbiter (MRO)

 The main objective of this orbiting probe is to look for traces of water on the surface of Mars. NASA launched the probe on Aug. 12, 2005; it reached Mars on March 10, 2006, after traveling 72 million miles (116 million km) in seven months. Although its mission was scheduled to end in 2010, the probe remains in good condition and continues to be operational.

Martian Orbit

Earth Orbit

Sun

Earth

Mars

5 SCIENTIFIC PHASE
The probe began the phase of analyzing the surface of Mars. It found indications of the presence of water.

4 MARS ARRIVAL
In March 2006 MRO passed under Mars's southern hemisphere. The probe began to decelerate.

3 TRAJECTORY CORRECTION
Four maneuvers were carried out to attain the right orbit.

1 LAUNCH
Launched on Aug. 12, 2005, from Cape Canaveral

2 CRUISING FLIGHT
The probe traveled 7.5 months before arriving at Mars.

72 million miles
(116 million km)

THE DISTANCE TRAVELED BY THE PROBE TO REACH MARS

TECHNICAL SPECIFICATIONS

Weight with fuel	4,800 pounds (2,180 kg)
Temperature rating of the panels	Down to -390° F (-200° C)
Launch rocket	Atlas V-401
Mission	11 years (with possible extension)
Cost	$ 720 million

2,270 pounds
(1,031 kg) WEIGHT ON EARTH

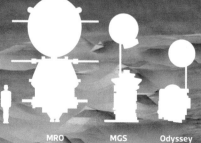

MRO   MGS   Odyssey

ANTICIPATED VOLUME OF DATA TRANSMISSION

DS1 (Comets)	15 Gigabytes
Odyssey (Mars)	1,012 Gigabytes
MGS (Mars)	1,759 Gigabytes
Cassini (Saturn)	2,550 Gigabytes
Magellan (Venus)	3,740 Gigabytes
MRO (Mars)	34,816 Gigabytes

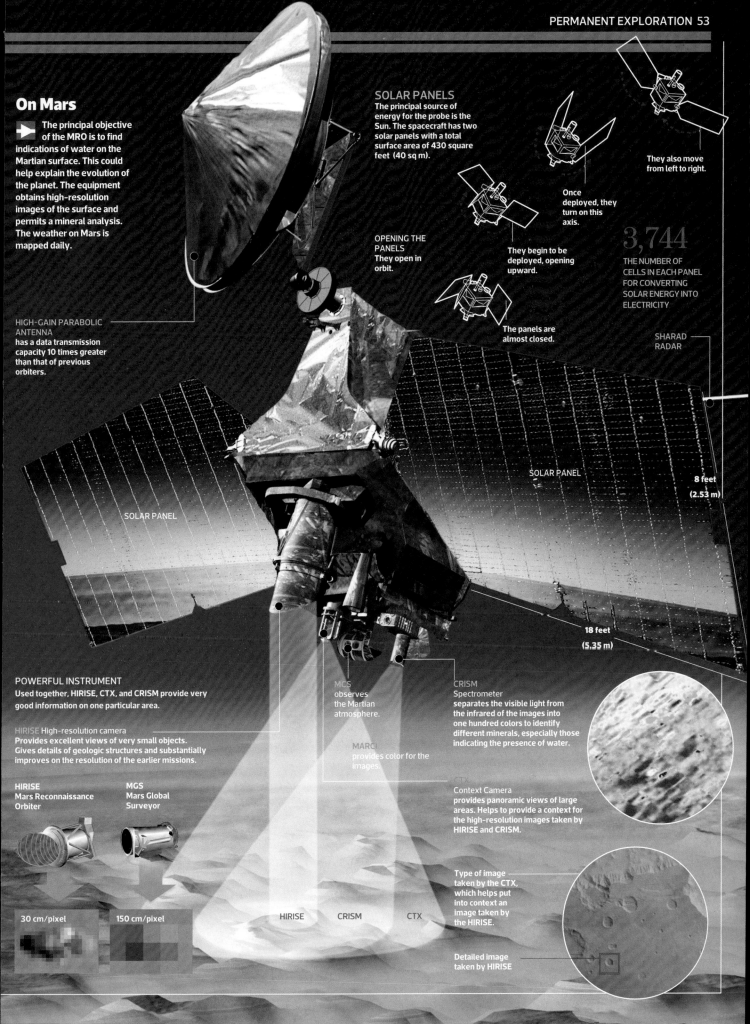

On Mars

The principal objective of the MRO is to find indications of water on the Martian surface. This could help explain the evolution of the planet. The equipment obtains high-resolution images of the surface and permits a mineral analysis. The weather on Mars is mapped daily.

HIGH-GAIN PARABOLIC ANTENNA has a data transmission capacity 10 times greater than that of previous orbiters.

SOLAR PANELS
The principal source of energy for the probe is the Sun. The spacecraft has two solar panels with a total surface area of 430 square feet (40 sq m).

OPENING THE PANELS
They open in orbit.

They begin to be deployed, opening upward.

The panels are almost closed.

Once deployed, they turn on this axis.

They also move from left to right.

3,744
THE NUMBER OF CELLS IN EACH PANEL FOR CONVERTING SOLAR ENERGY INTO ELECTRICITY

SHARAD RADAR

SOLAR PANEL

SOLAR PANEL

8 feet (2.53 m)

18 feet (5.35 m)

POWERFUL INSTRUMENT
Used together, HIRISE, CTX, and CRISM provide very good information on one particular area.

HIRISE High-resolution camera
Provides excellent views of very small objects. Gives details of geologic structures and substantially improves on the resolution of the earlier missions.

HIRISE
Mars Reconnaissance Orbiter

MGS
Mars Global Surveyor

MCS observes the Martian atmosphere.

MARCI provides color for the images.

CRISM
Spectrometer separates the visible light from the infrared of the images into one hundred colors to identify different minerals, especially those indicating the presence of water.

CTX
Context Camera provides panoramic views of large areas. Helps to provide a context for the high-resolution images taken by HIRISE and CRISM.

Type of image taken by the CTX, which helps put into context an image taken by the HIRISE.

Detailed image taken by HIRISE

30 cm/pixel

150 cm/pixel

HIRISE   CRISM   CTX

Martian Robots

Spirit and Opportunity—the twin robots that were launched in June 2003 from Earth and landed on Martian soil in January 2004—were designed to travel over the surface of the Red Planet. Both vehicles are part of NASA's Mars Exploration Rovers mission. They have tools that allow them to drill into rock and take samples of the soil to analyze their chemical composition. The robots are located on opposite sides of the planet to explore two uniquely different places. While Opportunity remains operative to this day, Spirit ceased comunications with Earth in 2010.

Water and Life on Mars

The main purpose of the mission conceived by NASA was to find indications whether there had ever been water on Mars. In Spirit's first mission, it was thought that small quantities of water might have seeped into the eroded rock fragments. The rocky Martian soil, it is believed, could have been affected by the action of water. So far, there is no evidence of the existence of living microorganisms. Between ultraviolet radiation and the oxidative nature of the soil, life on Mars is not currently possible. The question that remains is whether life might have existed at some time in the past or even today deep inside the Martian subsoil, where conditions for life might be more favorable.

TECHNICAL SPECIFICATIONS

Date of landing	Spirit: Jan. 3, 2004 Opportunity: Jan. 24, 2004
Cost of the mission	$ 820 million
Progress per day	330 feet (100 m)
Plutonium	Each spacecraft carries 0.01 ounces (2.8 g)
Useful life	More than two years

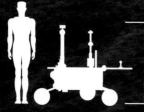

5 feet (1.50 m)

384 pounds
(174 kg)
WEIGHT ON EARTH

HOW IT GOT TO MARS
The voyage to Mars lasted seven months. Once inside the Martian atmosphere, parachutes were deployed to slow the descent.

Aeroshell

1 DECELERATION
The aeroshell kicks in at an altitude of 80 miles (130 km) above the surface in order to decelerate from 10,000 to 1,000 miles per hour (16,000 to 1,600 km/h.)

Parachutes

2 PARACHUTES
At six miles (10 km) above the surface, the parachutes open to reduce the speed of the descent.

3 FALL
The entry module is separated from the shield that protected it from the heat.

Entry module

4 ROCKETS
At 33 to 50 feet (10–15 m) above the surface, two rockets are ignited to slow the fall. Then the air bags are inflated to surround and protect the module.

Descent rockets

Vectran air bags

5 AIR BAGS
The module and the air bags separate themselves from the parachutes and fall to the Martian soil.

6 DESTINATION
The air bags deflate. The "petals" that protect the ship open. The vehicle exits.

7 INSTRUMENTS
The robot unfolds its solar panels, camera, and antenna mast.

Vectran air bags

The protective shi consists of three p and a central base

Photograph of the surface taken by Spirit

70,000 images
Obtained by Spirit in its first two years

Track and photograph taken by Opportunity

80,000 images
Obtained by Opportunity in its first two years on Mars

CAMERAS
Two navigational
cameras and two
panoramic cameras are
mounted on the mast.

Navigation
(NAVCAM)

Panoramic
(PANCAM)

Panoramic
(PANCAM)

PANCAM

360°

MAST

**VERTICAL
ANGLE OF
VISION**

NAVCAM

SOLAR PANELS

FRONT STEREO
CAMERA

OMNIDIRECTIONAL SHORTWAVE ANTENNA
transmits the information gathered by the robot to
the Control Center on Earth.

ELECTRONIC
MODULE

UHF
RADIO

INERTIAL
MEASUREMENT UNIT
provides information on
position relative to the x,
y, and z axes.

SOLAR PANELS
receive the light from
the Sun and transform
it into energy. The solar
battery can function
only with sunlight.

Generates about
140 watts
every four hours

ANTENNA

BATTERY

**ARM
FOLDED**

X-BAND
RADIO

**ARM
EXTENDED**

Abrasion
Tool

Microscope

MECHANICAL ARM
The most important
instruments for
analysis are located
at the extreme end
of the arm.

X-ray
Spectrometer

Mössbauer
Spectrometer

2 inches/second (5 cm/s)
Maximum velocity of forward motion on level ground

Stabilization

MOTION AND
PROPULSION

The robot has six wheels. Each one has
an individual electric motor that allows
it to make turns up to 360°, since both
the two front wheels and the two rear
wheels can be steered.

The propulsion
system allows
it to overcome
small obstacles.

OPERATIONAL CYCLES
The robot is programmed to function in cycles of 30 seconds.

0	10	20	30
ADVANCE		OBSERVATION	

A Home in Space

To live in space for long periods, it is necessary to have an environment that compensates for the lack of oxygen. Space stations have systems that provide oxygen to the crew and filter out the exhaled carbon dioxide. Life in a space station allows astronomers to study the effect of a long-term stay in space. Space stations also have laboratories for conducting scientific experiments. ●

SUPPLIES AND WASTE
The Russian spacecraft ATV docks with the ISS for unloading supplies and removing waste.

ATV

ISS

Space Giant

➤ The International Space Station (ISS) is the result of the integration of NASA's Freedom and the Russian Space Agency's Mir 2 projects. Construction began in 1998, and the large illustration shows what additions had been made by 2011. Various countries have contributed modules for the station. Its habitable surface area is equal to that of two Boeing 747s.

ORBIT
It carries out 16 orbits around the Earth each day at an altitude of 210 to 285 miles (335 to 460 km).

INTERNATIONAL SPACE STATION (ISS)

Habitable space	42,400 cubic feet (1,200 cu m)
Speed	17,200 mph (27,700 km/h)
Length	350 feet (108 m)
Panel surface area	43,000 square feet (4,000 sq m)
Laboratories	6

MANUFACTURER

USA   Russia   Japan   European Union

Zvezda Module

474,000 pounds
(215,000 kg)
WEIGHT ON EARTH

350 feet (108 m)

290 feet (88 m)

ISS   SKYLAB   MIR

41,912 pounds
(19,051 kg)
WEIGHT ON EARTH

ZVEZDA MODULE
The principal contribution by the Russians to the station. It is the first habitable compartment. It holds three to six astronauts.

Chest of Drawers

Beds

Shower

Kitchen and Dispensary

S6 Truss Segment (2009)

The floor and the roof have a different color to make orientation easier.

Deployable Solar Panels

Commanding Communication Zone

Connecting Node Between Modules

STAGES OF CONSTRUCTION

November 1998
Zarya Module
First section put into orbit. Provided energy in the first stages of ISS assembly. In December, the Unity Module connected passage between the living and work area modules. Contributed by the European Union.

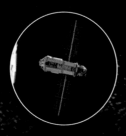

July 2000
Zvezda Module
The structural and functional center of the ISS. Entirely built and placed into orbit by the Russians. In November, the structural module P6 Truss incorporates radiators for dissipating the heat generated in the station.

February 2001
Laboratory Destiny
Holds 24 equipment racks. This is where scientific experiments in microgravity environments are performed. In November 2002, the P1 Truss was added opposite the S1 Truss as part of the integrated truss assembly. The truss radiator panels protect the ISS from the extreme temperatures.

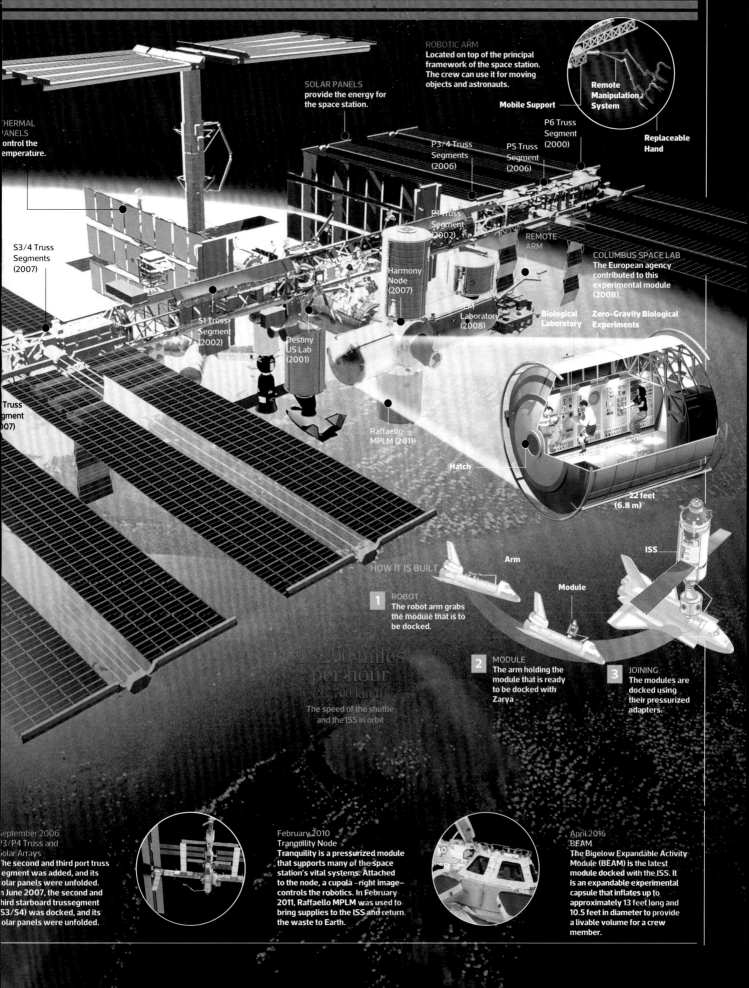

ROBOTIC ARM
Located on top of the principal framework of the space station. The crew can use it for moving objects and astronauts.

Remote Manipulation System

Mobile Support

Replaceable Hand

SOLAR PANELS
provide the energy for the space station.

THERMAL PANELS
control the temperature.

P6 Truss Segment (2000)

P3/4 Truss Segments (2006)

P5 Truss Segment (2006)

S3/4 Truss Segments (2007)

P1 Truss Segment (2002)

REMOTE ARM

COLUMBUS SPACE LAB
The European agency contributed to this experimental module (2008).

S1 Truss Segment (2002)

Harmony Node (2007)

JEM Laboratory (2008)

Biological Laboratory

Zero-Gravity Biological Experiments

Destiny US Lab (2001)

Truss egment 007)

Raffaello MPLM (2011)

Hatch

22 feet (6.8 m)

ISS

HOW IT IS BUILT

Arm

Module

1 ROBOT
The robot arm grabs the module that is to be docked.

2 MODULE
The arm holding the module that is ready to be docked with Zarya

3 JOINING
The modules are docked using their pressurized adapters.

17,200 miles per hour
(27,700 km/h)
The speed of the shuttle and the ISS in orbit

September 2006
P3/P4 Truss and Solar Arrays
The second and third port truss segment was added, and its solar panels were unfolded. In June 2007, the second and third starboard trussegment (S3/S4) was docked, and its solar panels were unfolded.

February 2010
Tranquility Node
Tranquility is a pressurized module that supports many of the space station's vital systems. Attached to the node, a cupola –right image– controls the robotics. In February 2011, Raffaello MPLM was used to bring supplies to the ISS and return the waste to Earth.

April 2016
BEAM
The Bigelow Expandable Activity Module (BEAM) is the latest module docked with the ISS. It is an expandable experimental capsule that inflates up to approximately 13 feet long and 10.5 feet in diameter to provide a livable volume for a crew member.

Spying on the Universe

Space telescopes such as the Hubble are artificial satellites put into orbit for observing different regions of the universe. Unlike telescopes on Earth, space telescopes are above the Earth's atmosphere. Therefore, they avoid the effects of atmospheric turbulence, which degrades the quality of telescopic images. Moreover, the atmosphere prevents the observation of the stars and other objects in certain wavelengths (especially the infrared), which substantially decreases what might be seen in the heavens. Space telescopes do not have to contend with light pollution, which is a problem for observatories near urban areas. ●

SHUTTER
During observations it opens to allow light to enter.

SECONDARY MIRROR
Located inside the telescope tube. Light reflects from the secondary mirror to the camera.

The Hubble Space Telescope

The Hubble was put into orbit on April 25, 1990, by NASA and ESA. It is an artificial satellite whose instruments are directed toward outer space. The telescope can be remotely controlled by astronomers at different locations. The telescope's computers point the telescope in the desired direction, and sensitive light detectors and cameras make the desired observations, in many cases producing impressive vistas of the cosmos. In 1993, because of a fault in the primary mirror, a corrective lens called COSTAR had to be installed to correct the focus of the telescope. COSTAR was replaced by the Cosmic Origins Spectograph in 2009.

TECHNICAL SPECIFICATIONS

Launch date	April 25, 1990
Orbital altitude	340 miles (547 km)
Orbital period	97 minutes
Type of telescope	Ritchey–Chretien Reflector
Organization	NASA and ESA
Decay estimation	2030–2040
Launch cost	$ 2 billion
Primary mirror diameter	8 feet (2.40 m)

46 feet (14 m)

14 feet (4.26 m)

24,500 pounds (11,100 kg)
WEIGHT ON EARTH

HOW IT CAPTURES IMAGES

The Hubble uses a system of mirrors that receive the light and cause it to converge until it reaches a focus.

Secondary Mirror

Primary Mirror

WFPC

Secondary Mirror

Primary Mirror

WFPC

Secondary Mirror

Primary Mirror

WFPC

A scientific instrument where the image is formed

KEY

Direction of the light

EXTERNAL LAYER
protects the telescope from external damage. During repair missions, the astronauts inspect it to look for particles and debris to be removed.

SOLAR PANEL

1 INCOMING LIGHT
The light enters through an aperture and is reflected in the primary mirror. Then the light converges toward a secondary mirror.

2 LIGHT REFLECTION
The rays coming from the primary mirror go to the secondary mirror, which reflects the light and returns it to the primary mirror.

3 IMAGE FORMED
The rays go through a hole in the primary mirror and are then concentrated in the focal plane, where they form an image.

OW IMAGES ARE TRANSMITTED

1 HUBBLE
Instructions for the desired observation are uploaded to the telescope, which then transmits the image or other observational data after the observation is completed.

2 TDRS SATELLITE
Receives the data from Hubble and sends them to a receiving antenna at the White Sands Test Facility in New Mexico.

3 EARTH
From New Mexico, data are transmitted to the Goddard Space Flight Center in Greenbelt, Maryland, where the information is analyzed.

IMAGES
The Hubble can photograph a large variety of objects—from galaxies and clusters of galaxies to stars on the verge of exploding (such as Eta Carinae) and planetary nebulae (such as the Cat's Eye).

STAR ETA CARINAE   **SUPERNOVA**   **CAT'S EYE NEBULA**

Because it is outside the atmosphere, Hubble photographs are sharper than those taken by terrestrial telescopes.

Other Telescopes

The Spitzer telescope, launched in August 2003, was designed to photograph very distant objects. SOHO, developed jointly by NASA and ESA, shows in detail the interactions between the Sun and the Earth. Chandra, launched in 1999, carries instruments that provide information about the position and energy of celestial X-ray sources.

HIGH-GAIN ANTENNA
receives orders from the Earth and sends back as TV signals the photos that the Hubble takes.

PRIMARY, OR PRINCIPAL, MIRROR
is 8 feet (2.4 m) in diameter; captures and focuses the light.

SOLAR PANEL
Energy is provided by directional solar antennas that convert sunlight into electricity.

SPITZER
observes the universe in infrared.

COSTAR
The optical device that corrected the defective original mirror of the Hubble. The device was put in place by space shuttle astronauts in 1993.

SOHO
Put into orbit in 1995, it takes images of the Sun.

CHANDRA
The only X-ray observatory

(WF/PC)
Primary electronic camera

ADVANCED CAMERA FOR SURVEYS

Space Junk

S ince the time that the first satellite (Sputnik) was launched in 1957, near space has become overcrowded with a large amount of debris. Satellite batteries that have exploded and parts of rockets and spacecraft still orbiting the Earth form a genuine cosmic garbage dump. These variously sized objects pose a danger to satellites and spacecraft because of the damage that would be caused by a collision—the particles move at speeds of 19,000 to 43,000 miles per hour (30,000 to 70,000 km/h).

Space Junk

Any object launched from Earth that is no longer useful but is still orbiting the Earth is considered space junk. Rockets used only once can remain in orbit, as do pieces of spacecraft or apparatuses ejected intentionally so that they would not enter the wrong orbit. Space junk can even include lost objects. In 1965, astronaut Edward White lost a glove, which kept orbiting the Earth for a month at 17,400 miles per hour (28,000 km/h).

SIZE OF SPACE JUNK

More than 17,000 objects and millions of tiny particles have been cataloged.

LESS THAN 0.4 INCH
(1 CM)
Very small particles cause superficial damage.
170,000,000+

FROM 0.4 TO 4 INCHES
(1-10 CM)
These particles can knock holes in satellites.
670,000+

MORE THAN 4 INCHES
(10 CM)
These objects can cause irreparable damage. These are the objects that are cataloged and tracked from Earth.
29,000+

OBJECTS IN SPACE BY COUNTRY

Since 1957, 25,000 objects have been launched into low orbit.

13,000

The approximate number of objects currently in orbit

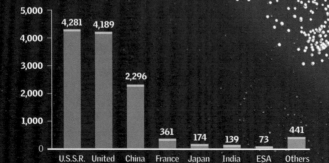

	U.S.S.R. /C.I.S.	United States	China	France	Japan	India	ESA	Others
	4,281	4,189	2,296	361	174	139	73	441

What Can Be Done?

One course of action would be to ensure that the junk is returned to Earth and not allowed to orbit around it. But the most that has been done is to remove satellite remains from Earth orbit.

SAIL
The sail would be deployed when the satellite has stopped functioning. Solar wind would push the satellite out of its orbit.

SPACE PROBE
Impacts the satellite, changing its orbit and pushing it in a predetermined direction.

CABLE
A cable drags the satellite to lower orbits, and the satellite disintegrates when it enters the atmosphere.

ORIGIN AND LOCATION

Ninety-five percent of the objects in space around the Earth are junk. NASA is studying rockets that do not get into orbit but fall to Earth to avoid generating more junk.

- **21% Inactive Satellites**
- **31% Rockets and Rocket Stages**
- **5% Active Satellites**
- **43% Satellite Fragments**

2,000 tons of junk in less than 1,200 miles (2,000 km)
Most of it consists of satellites that no longer operate and burnt-out stages of rockets.

LOW EARTH ORBIT
250 MILES (400 KM)
The ISS and the Hubble telescope are in low Earth orbits.

MEDIUM EARTH ORBIT
TYPICALLY 400 TO 1,200 MILES (700 TO 2,000 KM).
This is the orbit for telecommunications and environmental satellites.

GEOSTATIONARY ORBIT
22,250 MILES (35,800 KM)
Many spy satellites, which contribute to a significant part of the junk, are in this type of orbit.

HIGH ORBIT
62,000 MILES (100,000 KM)
Astronomical satellites operate at the highest altitudes.

- **JUNK**
- **IN OPERATION**
- **NUCLEAR SPILLS**

Visiting Other Worlds

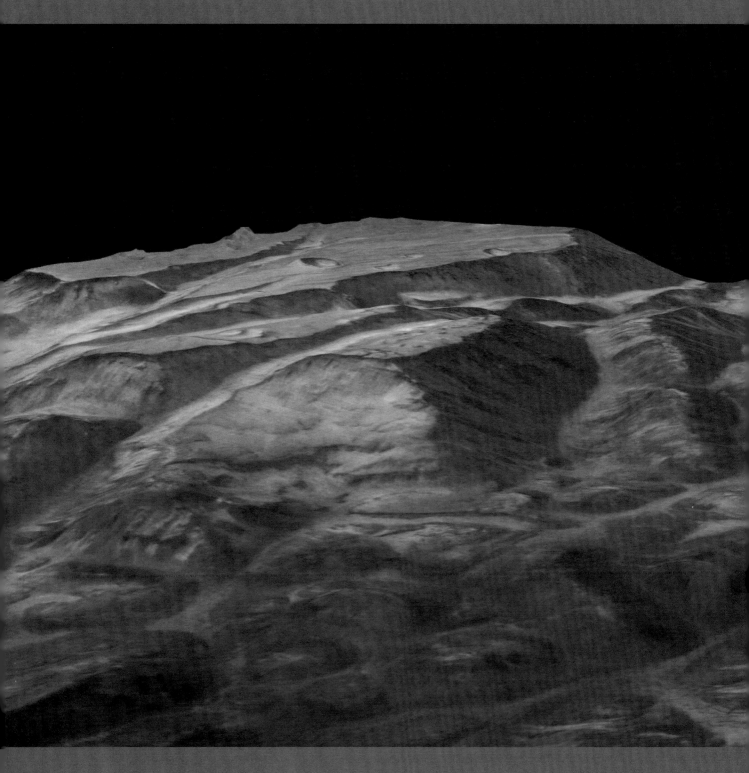

S pace exploration has allowed us access to worlds believed to have been inaccessible, and it has also helped the human race to become conscious of the planet Earth and the need to care for it. The future of planetary exploration appears promising. The next few years will see ever more interesting discoveries. Right now there

VALLES MARINERIS
The grand canyon of Mars is one of the most impressive geologic features of the entire solar system. It is some 2,400 miles (4,000 km) long and up to 6.2 miles (10 km) deep.

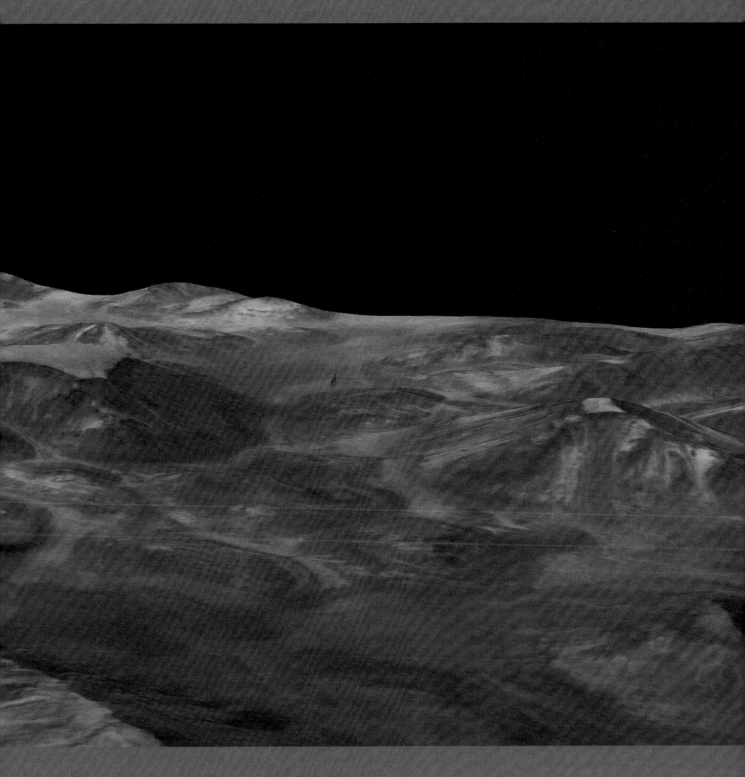

are spacecraft exploring or are on their way to explore other bodies of the solar system—Mars, Saturn, Jupiter, Venus, and even Pluto. The necessity of taking on large projects and traveling to sites ever farther away has always been with us. Therefore, each one of our accomplishments constitutes another step forward in our knowledge of space for the sake of all humanity. ●

Human Tracks

Ancient astronomers saw faint points of light that seemed to move among the stars. These objects were called planets, and each one of them was given the name of a god. In the 16th and 17th centuries, scientists came to recognize that the planets were physical bodies that revolved around the Sun. However, it was only recently, in the late 20th century, that technological advances permitted the direct study and the magnificent close-up photographs of the planets in the solar system. ●

The Planets

▲ From the sightings by Galileo to the construction of space stations capable of sheltering humans, interest in revealing the mysteries of the planets has never ceased. Detailed studies of the rings of Saturn, the patches of ice at the poles of Mars, the exploration of various comets and asteroids, and the flybys of the great moons of the major planets are among the most striking results of space exploration to date.

Pluto
Officially it is no longer considered a planet. Because of its small size, it has been called a dwarf planet since 2006.

Neptune
Visited only by Voyager 2, which took photographs in 1989

Uranus
In 1986 Voyager 2 flew by Uranus and took photographs.

Saturn
The Voyager and Cassini-Huygens missions have studied its rings in detail.

Jupiter
Some probes flew by the planet and took photographs. Galileo was in orbit for seven years, carrying out the most in-depth studies of its larger moons.

TITAN
The Huygens probe landed on the surface of Titan, the largest moon of Saturn.

It is believed to be a frozen volcano.

Enlarged area

The surface of the moon is in green and blue.

The atmosphere is in red.

Titan, a moon of Saturn

Enlarged area

350 photographs
of Titan's atmosphere and surface were obtained by ESA.

5 SUCCESSFUL MISSIONS

Mars, the Most Visited

A Mars landing was the top priority of the space agencies. The Red Planet, the one that most resembles Earth, might harbor or could have harbored life, according to experts.

In total, there have been 44 missions to Mars, of which

21
WERE SUCCESSFUL

MARTIAN SURFACE

Mons Olympus
Marinex Valley
Viking 1
Chryse Planitia
Pathfinder
Viking 2
Utopia Planitia
Isidis Planitia
Opportunity
Gusev
Spirit

This is the place where the most significant Mars missions landed.

The Sun

The Skylab space station obtained more than 150,000 images of the Sun between 1974 and 1979. Before it was decommissioned in 2009, the space probe Ulysses studied the Sun's poles and the effects of its magnetic field. The astronomical observatory SOHO is dedicated to studying the internal structure of the Sun and the origin of solar-wind particles. SOHO discovered three thousand comets, including a number that crashed into the Sun.

Mercury

The Mariner 10 mission explored the planet, and Messenger arrived there in 2011 and completed its mission in 2015.

Mariner 10 was able to photograph

57
percent of the planet.

Venus

The most important missions:
Venera (Soviet program), ESA's Venus Express, and Magellan (NASA)

12
MISSIONS LANDED ON VENUS.

Earth

The International Space Station (ISS) orbits the Earth with astronauts onboard. They carry out various experiments. Space telescopes such as the Hubble also orbit the Earth.

Earth's Moon

Enlarged area

KEY

The most significant missions to land on the Moon

xx Apollo
xx Luna
xx Surveyor

6
SUCCESSFUL MANNED MOON LANDINGS

The Moon

The obsession to carry out successful missions to the Moon began with the programs of the Soviet Union at the end of the 1950s in the context of the space race with the United States. It was President John F. Kennedy who in 1963 announced that the United States intended to put a man on the Moon before the end of the decade. In 1969, Apollo 11 landed on the Moon, beginning a series of successful manned missions.

FACE OF THE MOON VISIBLE FROM THE EARTH

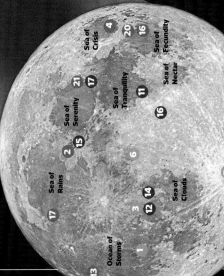

Sea of Rains
Sea of Serenity
Sea of Crisis
Sea of Tranquility
Sea of Nectar
Sea of Fecundity
Ocean of Storms
Sea of Clouds

Mars in the Sights

here was a time when it was thought that Mars, our closest neighbor, harbored life. Perhaps for this reason it is the planet that has been most explored by various spacecraft from the decade of the 1960s onward, and it is therefore the one we know the best, apart from the Earth. Mariner 9 in 1971 and Vikings 1 and 2 in 1976 revealed the existence of valleys and immense volcanic mountains. In 2001, the United States launched the Mars Odyssey mission, which indicated that liquid water exists at great depths.

Mars Odyssey Mission

▶ Named after *2001: A Space Odyssey*, the probe was launched by NASA from Cape Canaveral on April 7, 2001. It entered into Martian orbit in October of the same year. The Mars Odyssey was designed for a number of functions, such as taking images in the visible and infrared spectrum, studying the chemical composition of the planet's surface, and investigating the existence of possible sources of heat. One of its purposes was also to find traces of hydrogen and thus water on Mars. Finally, the Mars Odyssey was used in support tasks for other Mars missions, acting as a radio-signal repeater between Earth and probes on the Martian surface.

HINGE MECHANISM

GRS
Gamma-Ray Spectrometer
weighs 70 pounds (30 kg) and consumes 30 watts. It measures the abundance and distribution of 20 chemical elements on Mars.

THERMAL SHIELD

DOOR

SUPPORT

HEAD OF THE
GAMMA-RAY SENSOR

LAUNCH

APRIL 7, 2001
The spacecraft Mars Odyssey is launched toward Mars atop a Delta 2 rocket.

MARS ARRIVAL

OCT. 24, 2001
The spacecraft Mars Odyssey reaches the orbit of Mars and begins its scientific studies.

MARS
AT TIME OF LAUNCH

THE SUN

EARTH
AT TIME OF ARRIVAL

EARTH

MARS
ODYSSEY

MARS

CURRENT LOCATION OF THE ODYSSEY
It is orbiting Mars. It discovered the existence of ice, which was seen as a potential source of water for a future manned mission to the Red Planet.

MAY 2001
The spacecraft tests its cameras by sending an image of the Earth at a distance of 2 million miles (3 million km).

JUNE 2001
The gamma-ray spectrometer's protective hood is opened. The sensor begins to work.

JULY 2001
The probe activates its auxiliary engines to adjust its trajectory. The thrust lasts 23 seconds.

SEPTEMBER 2001
The probe begins to use the atmosphere to brake its speed, shape its orbit, and begin its mission.

TECHNICAL SPECIFICATIONS

Launch	April 7, 2001
Arrived on Mars	Oct. 24, 2001
Cost of the mission	$332 million
Weight	1,600 pounds (725 kg)
Useful life	10+ years

7 feet
(2.20 m)

8.5 feet (2.60 m)

Earth Seen from Mars

▶ Seen from Mars, the Earth is a magnificent blue star. From there, one can see the linked motions of the Earth and the Moon, as well as the combined phases of both. This photograph was taken by the Mars Odyssey in April 2006. Thanks to the spacecraft's infrared vision system, it was able to detect the temperatures on Earth, later confirmed by Earth-based sensors.

THE BLUE PLANET
A view of Earth from
Mars as recorded by
Mars Odyssey

Discovery

The new observations of Mars made by the Odyssey suggest that the north pole has about one third more underground ice than the south pole. Scientists also believe that microbial life could have developed on a planet other than Earth.

MARIE

An experiment measuring Mars's radiation environment

It weighs 7 pounds (3 kg) and consumes 7 watts. It is supposed to measure radiation produced by the Sun or other stars and celestial bodies that reach the orbit of Mars.

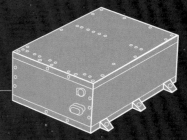

7 MONTHS

The time it took
Mars Odyssey to
reach its target

SOLAR
PANELS

HIGH-GAIN
ANTENNA

NEUTRON
SPECTROMETER

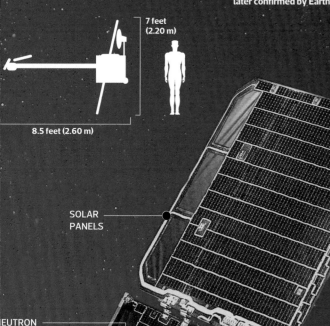

VIDEOCAMERAS

NEUTRON
ENERGY
DETECTOR

UHF ANTENNA

SURFACE
OF MARS

Unlike the Earth, basalt
dunes are common on
Mars. The surface is
flat and reminiscent
of a desert.

THEMIS

Thermal Emission Imaging System

Weighing 2,000 pounds (911 kg) and consuming 14 watts, this camera operates in the infrared spectrum. Its images allow conclusions to be drawn about the composition of the surface based on the spectrum of the infrared image and on the recorded temperature.

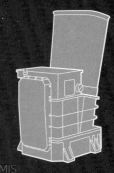

Jupiter in Focus

The fifth planet of the solar system was visited by Pioneer 1 and 2, Voyager 1 and 2, and Cassini. However, the most significant visitor was Galileo, launched by NASA on Oct. 18, 1989. Galileo consisted of an orbiter and an atmospheric probe. After a long voyage, the atmospheric probe penetrated some 125 miles (200 km) into the atmosphere of Jupiter on Dec. 7, 1995, transmitting data about the atmosphere's chemical composition and Jupiter's meteorological activity. The orbiter continued sending information until it crashed into the gaseous giant on Sept. 21, 2003.

Trajectory

Galileo was designed to study the atmosphere of Jupiter, its satellites, and the magnetosphere of the planet. To get there, it did not use a direct path but had to perform an assisted trajectory, passing by Venus on Feb. 10, 1990. Then it flew by the Earth twice and arrived at Jupiter on Dec. 7, 1995. The probe succeeded in sending information of unprecedented quality with a low-gain antenna about the satellites of Jupiter, its moon Europa, and various examples of volcanic activity in its moon Io. It also contributed to the discovery of 21 new satellites around Jupiter. The mission was deactivated in 2003, and the vehicle was sent to crash into the planet. The purpose of this termination was to avoid future collision with its moon Europa that might have contaminated its ice; scientists believe that extraterrestrial microscopic life may have evolved on Europa.

ATMOSPHERIC PROBE
Released when Galileo arrived at Jupiter. It was used to study the planet's atmosphere.

LOW-GAIN ANTENNA

BOOSTERS

SOLAR PANEL

LOW-GAIN ANTENNA

14 years

was the duration of the Galileo mission—from October 1989 to September 2003.

MAGNETIC SENSORS

LAUNCH
OCT. 18, 1989

Galileo was launched by NASA from the space shuttle Atlantis with Jupiter as its destination.

EARTH FLYBYS
DECEMBER 1990/AUGUST 1992

Galileo passes by the Earth on two occasions to get the necessary boost toward Jupiter.

ARRIVAL AT JUPITER
DEC. 7, 1995

Galileo arrived at Jupiter and began the scientific studies that continued until 2003. It completed 35 orbits around the planet.

VENUS FLYBY
FEB. 10, 1990

Galileo transmitted data from Venus.

IDA FLYBY
AUG. 28, 1993

Galileo came close to the asteroid Ida.

GASPRA FLYBY
OCT. 29, 1991

Galileo approached the asteroid 951 Gaspra.

SURFACE OF EUROPA

The areas in red consist of dirty ice formed by water mixed with rocky material that slowly seeped into the ice and once there began to freeze. The "cracks" are caused by the breakup of the ice.

Galileo

▶ In spite of its mission being plagued by technical problems, Galileo provided astronomers with a huge amount of information during its 35 orbits around Jupiter. The useful life of the probe, which cost $1.5 billion, extended five years longer than planned. The probe contributed to the discovery of 21 new satellites around Jupiter. Galileo sent large amounts of data and 14,000 images to Earth. It found traces of salt water on the surface of the moon Europa and evidence that it probably also exists on the moons Ganymede and Callisto. Likewise, it provided information about volcanic activity on the moon Io. It also showed an almost invisible ring around Jupiter consisting of meteorite dust. From the moment it was launched until its disintegration, the spacecraft traveled almost 2.9 billion miles (4.6 billion km) with barely 2,000 pounds (925 kg) of combustible fuel. More than 800 scientists worked on the project.

TECHNICAL SPECIFICATIONS

Date of arrival	Dec. 7, 1995
Cost of the mission	$1.5 billion
Useful life	14 years
Weight without the probe	4,900 pounds (2,223 kg)
Organization	NASA

23 feet (7 m)

20 feet (6.2 m)

ATMOSPHERE OF JUPITER

Composed of 90 percent hydrogen and 10 percent helium. The colors of the atmospheric clouds depend on their chemical composition. The clouds spread with the violent turbulence of the atmospheric winds.

IO

is one of the moons of Jupiter. It is notable for its brilliant color, which is caused by various sulfur compounds on its surface. Io is 417,000 miles (671,000 km) from Jupiter and was discovered by Galileo in 1610.

DESCENT TO JUPITER

1 Galileo released the atmospheric probe, which descended into Jupiter's atmosphere. The probe was provided with a deceleration and a descent module.

2 The deceleration module included protective heat shields and thermal control hardware for the phases of the mission leading up to the entry into the atmosphere.

DECELERATION MODULE

ANTENNA

PARACHUTES

DESCENT MODULE

3 A parachute 8 feet (2.5 m) in diameter was used to separate the descent module from the deceleration module and to control the velocity of the fall during the atmospheric descent phase.

PARACHUTES

4 The descent module carried six scientific instruments. During its 57 minutes of active life, the probe performed all the measurements and experiments that had been planned by the scientists.

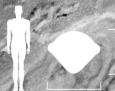

Atmospheric Probe

▶ Once Galileo arrived at the planet Jupiter, it released a small probe that fell through the atmosphere. This descent probe carried scientific instruments and the subsystems required to keep them active and transmit the data to the orbiter for storage for later transmittal to Earth. During its 57 minutes of active life in the Jovian atmosphere, the descent provided a number of discoveries, including a surprising lack of water in the upper layers of the Jovian clouds.

TECHNICAL SPECIFICATIONS

Entry into the atmosphere	Dec. 7, 1995
Active life	57 minutes
Weight	750 pounds (339 kg)
Organization	NASA

3 feet (0.86 m)

4 feet (1.25 m)

A View of Saturn

The longed-for return to Saturn was the result of a scientific alliance between NASA and the European Space Agency (ESA). On Oct. 15, 1997, after a number of years of development, the fruit of this collaboration lifted off toward this enormous gas giant. The mission of Cassini, the mother ship, was the exploration of Saturn. It carried a smaller probe, Huygens, that was to land on Saturn's largest moon, Titan, and transmit images and sounds from the surface. The Huygens probe accomplished this prodigious feat, demonstrating once again the capacity of humans to respond to the challenge of frontiers.

THE RINGS OF SATURN

are a conglomerate of ice particles and powdered rock orbiting the planet. The rings are 4.5 billion years old.

Trajectory

The trajectory of Cassini-Huygens was long and complicated, because it included strategic flybys of Venus (1998 and 1999), Earth (1999), and Jupiter (2000). Each one of these encounters was used to increase the craft's velocity and to send the spacecraft in the appropriate direction (a maneuver known as a gravity assist). Finally, and after almost seven years, traveling some 2.2 billion miles (3.5 billion km), the spacecraft arrived at its destination. It brought an end to the long wait since the last visit of a probe to Saturn—the 1981 flyby by Voyager 2.

VENUS 1
APRIL 1998
Cassini flies by Venus at an altitude of 180 miles (284 km).

THE EARTH
AUGUST 1999
Cassini flies by the Earth at an altitude of 730 miles (1,171 km).

SATURN
JUNE 2004
After seven years en route, Cassini arrives at Saturn and enters into an orbit around it.

EXTENSION FOR THE MAGNETOMETER

VENUS 2
JUNE 1999
Cassini flies by Venus at an altitude of 380 miles (600 km).

JUPITER
DECEMBER 2000
Cassini flies by Jupiter at an altitude of 6,042,000 miles (9,723,896 km).

TRAJECTORY FOR SATURN AND TITAN
Here is a drawing showing some of the 74 orbits planned for the mission.

Meeting between Huygens and Titan

Equatorial Rotation

Upward Trajectory

Titan's Orbit

Initial Orbit

Saturn
Seen from the North Pole

Occultation Orbit

Equatorial Rotation

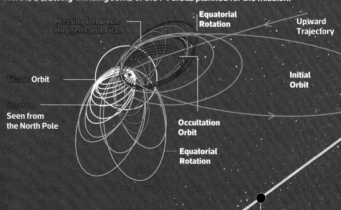

Spacecraft Thruster (1 of 2)

PHOTO OF JUPITER AND IO
The moon Io, the closest to the planet Jupiter, is composed of a rocky silicate material. The nucleus has a radius of 560 miles (900 km) and may consist of iron. This is the photo taken by the Cassini probe.

ANTENNA FOR THE RADIO SUBSYSTEMS AND THE PLASMA PROBES (1 OF 3)

Cassini-Huygens

The information sent by Huygens and relayed by Cassini took 67 minutes to travel from Saturn to the Earth. Although it could only see a small section of Titan, the apparatus was able to answer some key questions. For example, the probe did not find liquid, but it did find signs that the surface had a crust that was hard on top and soft underneath, which was flooded from time to time. Investigators said that Titan could have very infrequent precipitation, but when it occurred it could be abundant and cause flooding. Moreover, it appears that some of the conditions for life to arise exist on Titan, although it is too cold for life to have started.

TECHNICAL SPECIFICATIONS

Date of launch	Oct. 15, 1997
Begins Saturn orbit	July 1, 2004
Closest approach	11,800 miles (19,000 km)
Weight	12,300 pounds (5,600 kg)
Organizations	NASA and ESA

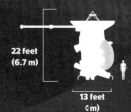

22 feet
(6.7 m)

13 feet
(4 m)

12,300 pounds (5,600 kg)
WEIGHT ON EARTH

HIGH-GAIN ANTENNA

LOW-GAIN ANTENNA (1 OF 2)

RADAR

TELESCOPES

GTR (RADIOISOTOPE THERMOELECTRIC GENERATOR)

770 pounds (350 kg)
WEIGHT ON EARTH

Descent onto Titan

On Jan. 14, 2005, the six instruments of Huygens worked without pause during the two-and-a-half-hour descent. They confirmed, for example, that the gaseous blanket that surrounds Titan consists primarily of nitrogen and that its yellowish color is caused by the presence of complex hydrocarbons, which are formed when sunlight breaks down atmospheric methane. The thermometer measured –400° F (–203° C) at an altitude of 31 miles (50 km), which was the lowest temperature recorded during the entire mission.

1 SEPARATION
The Huygens probe separates from Cassini.

2 DESCENT
lasted 150 minutes and came within 790 miles (1,270 km) of the surface.

3 FIRST PARACHUTE
helped decelerate the probe during its fall.

4 SECOND PARACHUTE
replaced the first.

THE SURFACE OF TITAN

is obscured by a deep layer of clouds. It is possible that many chemical compounds similar to those that preceded life on Earth exist in a frozen state at high altitudes.

5 THIRD PARACHUTE
replaced the second.

6 DEPLOYS ITS LANDING FEET
The probe prepares for touchdown.

7 IMPACT ON THE SURFACE
The spacecraft strikes the surface of Titan.

TECHNICAL SPECIFICATIONS: HUYGENS

Date of release	Dec. 25, 2004
Weight	703 pounds (319 kg)
Organizations	NASA and ESA
Date of landing	Jan. 14, 2005
Descent by parachute	2.5 hours

PLACEMENT OF HUYGENS ON CASSINI

22 feet
(6.8 m)

9 feet
(2.7 m)

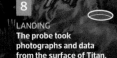

8 LANDING
The probe took photographs and data from the surface of Titan.

Toward Venus and Pluto

The New Horizons mission, launched by NASA in January 2006, is a voyage that will carry the spacecraft to the limits of the solar system and beyond. The most important goal of the voyage is to visit Pluto, a dwarf planet (a designation made in 2006 by the International Astronomical Union). New Horizons was able to complete this task in 2015, making it the first ship to complete a flyby of Pluto. New Horizons will continue its voyage toward the region of the solar system known as the Kuiper belt. It is estimated to arrive in 2019.

New Horizons Mission

An unmanned space mission by NASA whose destination is to explore Pluto and the Kuiper belt. The probe was launched from Cape Canaveral on Jan. 19, 2006. It flew past Jupiter in February 2007 to take advantage of the planet's gravity and increase its speed. It arrived at Pluto on July 14, 2015 and became the first probe to explore the dwarf planet. The data provided by this mission will help scientists to study the form and structure of Pluto and its satellite Charon, analyze the variability of the temperature on Pluto's surface, look for additional satellites around Pluto, and analyze high-resolution images. The probe is now on its way to explore more objects in the Kuiper belt. The power source for the spacecraft is a radioisotope thermoelectric generator.

RADIOISOTOPE GENERATOR
provides energy for propulsion of the spacecraft.

LOW-GAIN ANTENNA
Auxiliary to the high-gain antenna, which it can replace in case of breakdown

LAUNCH
JAN. 19, 2006
The New Horizons probe is launched from Cape Canaveral toward Jupiter, Pluto, and the Kuiper belt.

JUPITER FLYBY
FEBRUARY 2007
The probe flies by Jupiter to take advantage of the gravity of the planet on its journey toward Pluto.

KUIPER FLYBY
2019
The probe flies by one or more Kuiper belt objects.

INTERSECTING THE ORBIT OF MARS
APRIL 7, 2006
The probe traverses the Martian orbit.

ARRIVAL AT PLUTO
JULY 14, 2015
New Horizons flies by Pluto and its moon Charon. It sends to Earth data about the surface, the atmosphere, and the climate.

SPECTROMETER 1

will study the interaction of Pluto with the solar wind to determine if it possesses a magnetosphere.

The Spacecraft

The central structure of New Horizons is an aluminum cylinder that weighs 1,025 pounds (465 kg), of which 66 pounds (30 kg) are accounted for by scientific instruments. All its systems and devices have backups. The spacecraft carries a sophisticated guidance-and-control system for orientation. It has cameras to follow the stars and help find the right direction. These cameras have a star map with 3,000 stars stored in their memory. Ten times each second, one of the cameras takes a wide-angle image of space and compares it with the stored map.

ANTENNA

High-gain, 7 feet (2.2 m) in diameter, its purpose is to communicate with the Earth.

RADIOMETER

measures the atmospheric composition and temperature.

TELESCOPIC CAMERA

will map Pluto and gather high-quality geologic data.

THRUSTERS

The spacecraft carries six thrusters to increase its speed during flight.

TECHNICAL SPECIFICATIONS	
Launched	Jan. 19, 2006
Flyby	Pluto
Cost	$650 million
Weight	1,025 pounds (465 kg)
Organization	NASA

2.5 feet (0.70 m)

7 feet (2.1 m)

2015

The spacecraft New Horizons arrived at Pluto on July 14, 2015.

The Venus Express Mission

Venus is a little smaller than the Earth and has a dense atmosphere. Because it is located at slightly more than 67 million miles (108 million km) from the Sun , it receives almost twice the solar energy as the surface of the Earth. The Venus Express was the first mission of the European Space Agency to Venus. The aim of the Venus Express mission was to study the atmosphere, the plasma medium, the surface of the planet, and surface-atmosphere interactions. It was launched from the Baikonur cosmodrome on Nov. 9, 2005. The mission lasted nine years. The spacecraft entered into orbit on April 11, 2006 and concluded its mission in Dec. 2014.

LAUNCH
Nov. 9, 2005

ARRIVAL AT VENUS
April 11, 2006

TECHNICAL SPECIFICATIONS	
Launch	Nov. 9, 2005
Cost	$260 million
Weight	2,700 pounds (1,240 kg)
Organization	ESA

6 feet (1.8 m)

5 feet (1.5 m)

SPECTROMETER 1
measures the atmospheric temperature.

SPECTROMETER 2
operates on ultraviolet rays..

SOLAR PANELS
capture the energy from the Sun that powers the mission.

CAMERA
captures images in the ultraviolet.

MAGNETOMETER
measures magnetic fields and their direction.

HIGH-GAIN ANTENNA
transmits data to Earth.

Closer to the Sun

The space probe Ulysses was launched from the space shuttle on Oct. 6, 1990. It completed its first orbit around the Sun in 1997 and carried out one of the most in-depth studies ever about our star. The probe's orbits allowed it to study the heliosphere at all latitudes, from the equator to the poles, in both the northern and southern hemispheres of the Sun . The joint NASA and ESA mission was the first to orbit around the poles of the Sun. It orbited the Sun at 10 miles per second (15.4 km/s). Ulysses was decomissioned in 2009.

SWOOPS
An instrument that studies the ionic composition of the solar wind and the particle material

PASSES OVER THE SOLAR NORTH POLE
June-October 1995
September-December 2001
November 2007-January 2008

1 Beginning of the first orbit: **1992**

2 Beginning of the second orbit: **1998**

3 Beginning of the third orbit: **2004**

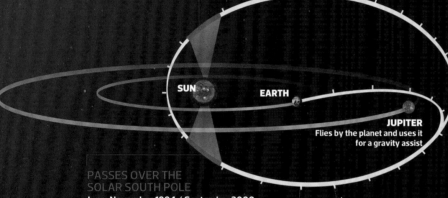

SUN   EARTH

JUPITER
Flies by the planet and uses it for a gravity assist

PASSES OVER THE SOLAR SOUTH POLE
June-November 1994 / September 2000
January 2001 / November 2006-April 2007

100 days

HIGH-GAIN ANTENNA
The antenna used for communication with Earth stations.

FIRST ORBIT

ORDER OF THE HELIOSPHERE
Ulysses completed its first solar orbit in December 1997 after having passed over the north pole. The heliosphere's structure was seen to be bimodal—that is, the solar winds were faster at greater inclinations of the orbit (beginning at 36°). During the first orbit, there was relatively little solar activity.

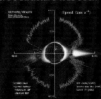

SECOND ORBIT

HELIOSPHERE CHAOS
The information obtained by the Ulysses probe in the year 2000 showed a structural change in the solar wind during the period of maximum solar activity. Ulysses did not detect patterns in which wind speed corresponded with inclination, and in general the solar wind was slower and more variable.

THIRD ORBIT

CHANGES IN THE MAGNETIC FIELD
After having survived the difficult pounding of the solar activity during its second orbit, the Ulysses probe began a third orbit around the Sun's poles in February 2007. Solar activity was expected to be at a minimum, as it was in 1994, but the poles of the magnetic field are reversed.

THERMOELECTRIC RADIOISOTOPE GENERATOR
provides electric energy for propelling the spacecraft in space.

DUST
An internal device to study the energy composition of the heliosphere's particles and cosmic dust.

RADIAL ANTENNA
contains four devices for different experiments.

GRM
A device that studies the gamma rays emitted by the Sun

VHM
A device for studying the magnetic field of the heliosphere

URAP
is used to measure the radio waves and plasma in the solar wind.

Solar Wind and the Earth

Thanks to its intense nuclear activity the Sun expels a million tons of particles per second into space. This particle flow forms a low-density plasma that extends the Sun's magnetic field and interacts with the Earth's magnetosphere. The area where the solar wind no longer has an effect is called the heliopause.

SHOCKWAVE
The solar wind collides with the Earth's magnetic field.

SOLAR WIND

HI-SCALE
Device designed to measure the energy present in ions and electrons of the interplanetary medium

BANDS OF MAGNETIC FIELD
Generated by the bipolar characteristic of the Earth

REACTION TANK
A tank of fuel used for correcting the probe's orbit

ANTENNA CABLE CONTROL
A device onboard the spacecraft to change the position of the antennas

GOLD COVERING
It serves as insulation to help maintain the spacecraft's instruments at a temperature below 95° F (35° C) while the fuel is kept at a temperature above 41° F (5° C).

ANTENNA CABLE
There is one on each side of the spacecraft. They are deployed after liftoff.

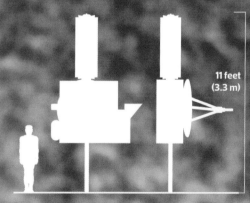

11 feet
(3.3 m)

10 miles
(15.4 km) per second
THE VELOCITY REACHED BY THE ULYSSES PROBE

TECHNICAL SPECIFICATIONS: ULYSSES	
Launch date	Oct. 6, 1990
Weight when launched	815 pounds (370 kg)
Weight of the instruments	1,200 pounds (550 kg)
Orbital inclination	80.2° with respect to the ecliptic
Organization	NASA and ESA (joint mission)

The Road Beyond

The space probes Voyager 1 and 2 were launched by NASA to study the outer solar system. Voyager 1 was launched on Sept. 5, 1977, and flew by Jupiter in 1979 and Saturn in 1980. Voyager 2 lifted off on Aug. 20, 1977, then flew by Jupiter and Saturn to reach Uranus in 1986 and Neptune in 1989. Voyager 2 is the only probe that has visited both of these planets. Both probes have now become the furthest distant artificial instruments ever sent into space by humans. ●

PIONEER 10 AND 11

In 1973 Pioneer 10 became the first spacecraft to fly by Jupiter. It was followed by Pioneer 11, which made a flyby of Jupiter in 1974 and Saturn in 1979. Pioneer 11 stopped working in 1995. Signals were received from Pioneer 10 until 2003.

THE FRONTIER OF THE SOLAR SYSTEM

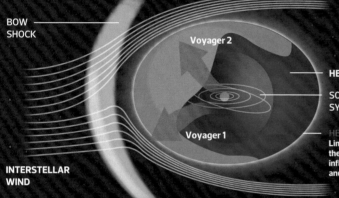

BOW SHOCK

Voyager 2

HELIOSPHERE

SOLAR SYSTEM

Voyager 1

HELIOPAUSE
Limit zone between the area of influence of the Sun and outer space

INTERSTELLAR WIND

Voyager 2

Voyager 1

TRAJECTORY
The Voyager probe passed by Jupiter in 1979 and by Saturn in 1980. The Voyager 2 did the same and arrived at Uranus in 1986 and Neptune in 1989. Both are still active.

- EARTH
- JUPITER
- SATURN
- URANUS
- NEPTUNE

Looking for the Heliopause

▶ With Voyagers 1 and 2 leaving the Solar System, the project was renamed the Interstellar Voyager Mission. Both probes continue to study the magnetic fields they detect, looking for the heliopause—that is, the limit between the area of the Sun's influence and interstellar space. Once that frontier has been passed, the Voyagers will be able to measure waves that escape the solar magnetic field, beginning with the so-called "bow shock," a zone where the solar wind diminishes abruptly because of the disappearance of the solar magnetic field. It is hoped that the Voyagers will continue to be active for at least 10 years.

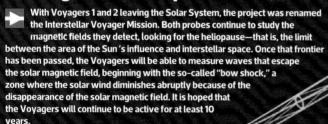

14,000 days

have passed since Voyager 1 was launched into space. During this time, it discovered 21 new satellites of the four planets studied; it proved that the rings of Saturn consist of particles of ice; it discovered the rings of Neptune; and it determined the character of the magnetic field of Uranus.

MILESTONES OF THE VOYAGE

1977
LAUNCHES
The space probes Voyager 1 and 2 were launched by NASA from Cape Canaveral. They then began a long and successful mission that continues today.

1977
PHOTO OF THE EARTH AND THE MOON
On September 5, Voyager 1 sent photographs of the Earth and the Moon, demonstrating that it was working perfectly.

1986
ENCOUNTER WITH URANUS
On January 24, Voyager 2 arrived at Uranus. It sent photographs of the planet to the Earth and sent data on its satellites, rings, and magnetic fields.

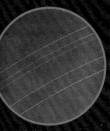

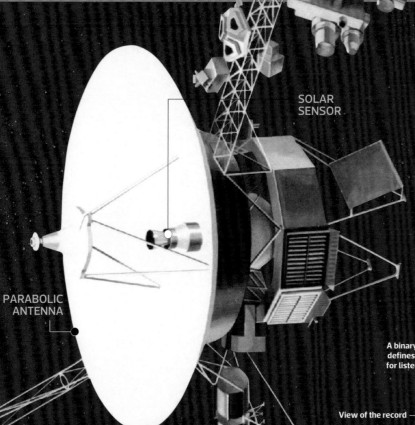

SOLAR
SENSOR

PARABOLIC
ANTENNA

Golden Record

The Voyagers carried the recorded greetings of humanity in a golden, 12-inch record. Each spacecraft had one, with information about life on Earth, photographs, music of Mozart, Bach, and Beethoven, greetings in more than 50 languages, and the brain waves of a woman (Ann Druyan, the wife of the now-deceased astronomer Carl Sagan, who supervised this collection). If the message finds anyone who can respond, it will be, in the words of Sagan, "humanity's most important discovery."

WHAT THE RECORD IS LIKE

A binary code that defines the speed for listening to the sounds

Cartridge

A representation of the waves produced by the video signal

View of the record

Binary code that marks the time

Profile of the cartridge

Scanner trigger

Video image

If the disk is decoded, the first image will appear in the circle.

This diagram defines the location of our Sun by using 14 directional lines.

Represents the two stages of the hydrogen atom

COMMUNICATION WITH THE EARTH

The high-gain antenna, 12 feet (3.7 m) in diameter, is located in the upper part of the central body.

The antenna must point in the exact direction.

ANTENNA
A sensor records the position of the Sun.

If the antenna is misdirected, the information will not get to its destination.

TECHNICAL SPECIFICATIONS: VOYAGER 1 AND 2

Launch date	1977
Useful life	60 years
Weight	1,800 pounds (815 kg)
Source of energy	Plutonium
Organization	NASA

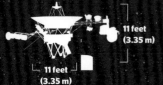

11 feet
(3.35 m)

11 feet
(3.35 m)

1,800 pounds (815 kg)
WEIGHT ON EARTH

1987
OBSERVATION OF A SUPERNOVA
Supernova 1987A appeared in the Large Magellanic Cloud. It was photographed with great clarity by the space probe Voyager 2.

1989
COLOR PHOTO OF NEPTUNE
Voyager 2 is the first space probe to observe Neptune. It also photographed its largest moon, Triton, from close up.

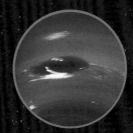

1998
PASSES PIONEER 10
Pioneer 10, launched in 1973, was the farthest spacecraft from Earth until Feb. 17, 1998, when Voyager 1, not launched until 1977 but traveling faster, passed Pioneer 10 in terms of distance.

Applied Astronautics

S pace tourism is ready to take off, and in the next decades it will become an adventure within the reach of many pocketbooks. In 2004, SpaceShipOne became the first private manned vehicle to reach near outer space and to remain outside the atmosphere for three minutes. Then it made a problem-free landing in the California desert. The project cost $20

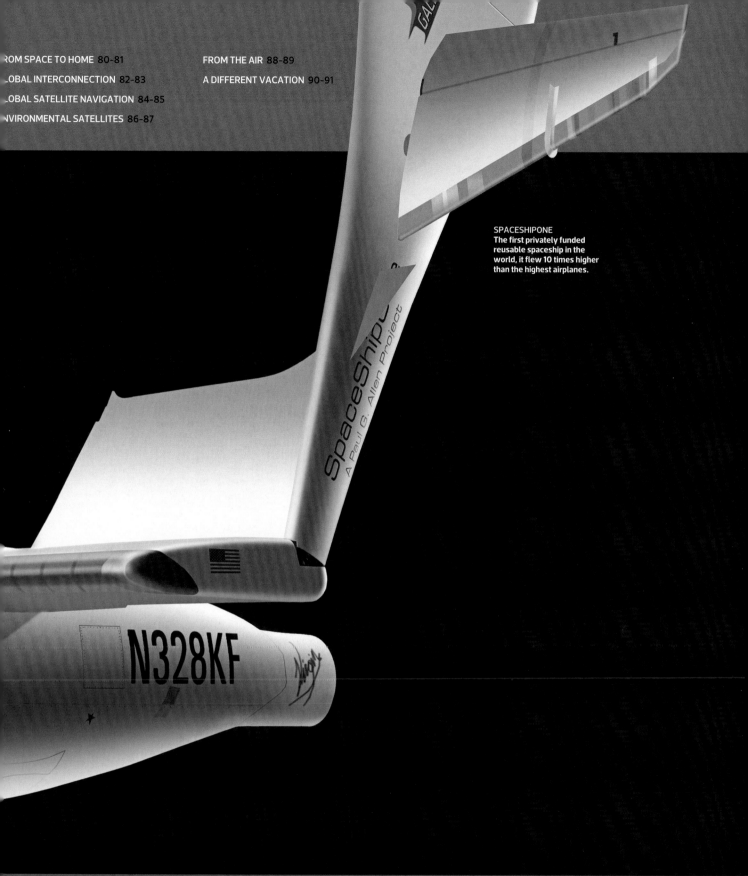

SPACESHIPONE
The first privately funded reusable spaceship in the world, it flew 10 times higher than the highest airplanes.

million and was financed by one of the founders of Microsoft. Many people made expensive reservations to fly in the craft and experience microgravity. It bears mentioning that manned space programs led to the development of various technologies, including cordless devices, implanted cardiac defibrillators, and digital imaging, to mention just a few. ●

From Space to Home

Space has been a laboratory for investigating and developing new technologies and methods, the applications of which have found a place in daily life. Various devices, foods, clothes, materials, and utensils have been tested in space under extreme conditions and have become useful in improving our lives. Scientists say that the technological innovations of the next 50 years will change society in such a way that a change in overall thinking will be necessary to assimilate them.

Intelligent Clothing

Clothing with computers and other technological capabilities incorporated into them has passed from the fiction of futurist movies to a reality that is getting closer and closer. New clothing has been designed to demonstrate how electronics can transform something to wear into intelligent, biometric clothing that responds to surrounding environmental conditions and to the wearer's vital signs. Thanks to the new types of cloth, scientists are already talking about garments to prevent diseases.

MAMAGOOSE

Mamagoose pajamas are used to monitor infants when they are at home sleeping. These pajamas have five sensors on the chest and stomach. Three of them monitor the heartbeat and the other two the respiration. The pajamas detect and warn of possible sudden infant death syndrome. The system is similar to the one used to continuously monitor the vital signs of the astronauts in space.

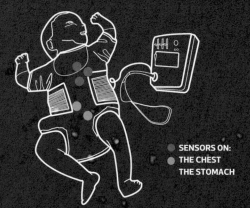

SENSORS ON:
THE CHEST
THE STOMACH

Domestic Uses

Frequent space travel has brought the application of new technologies to the home environment. Such is the case with microwave ovens and dehydrated food. It is only recently that they became part of the daily routine of the family in the home.

VELCRO

A system for rapidly joining and separating two parts that was created by George de Mestral in 1941

FOOD

The explorers dry their food and keep it in a cool place. The menu includes dried fruit, smoked turkey, flour tortillas, soy-milk cheese, walnuts, and peanuts.

MICROWAVE OVENS

Became popular in the United States in the 1970s. They allow rapid cooking or reheating of food thanks to the application of electromagnetic waves.

Air Purifiers

Air purifiers are designed to reduce the concentration of bacteria in the home and are beneficial for people suffering from allergies or asthma. Air purifiers are portable and can be carried from one room to another.

1 PHASE 1
The purifier takes in contaminated air with allergens.

2 PHASE 2
A filter processes the contaminated air.

3 PHASE 3
The purifier returns the pure air to the environment.

CONTAMINATED AIR

PURE AIR

POLYCARBONATE

Compacted polycarbonate used in layers has high resistance to impact. It replaces glass and is also used in eyeglasses.

KEVLAR

A synthetic polyamide, used in especially protective clothing, such as bulletproof vests, equipment for extreme sports, and blankets.

SILICONE

A polymer made of silicon. Used as a lubricants and adhesives and for waterproofing, ice-cube trays, and medical applications.

TEFLON

The common name of polytetrafluoroethylene. The special quality of this material is that it is almost inert—that is, it does not react with other chemical substances except under very special conditions. Another quality is its impermeability, maintaining its qualities in humid environments. Its best-known property is antisticking. It is used as a coating material on rockets and airplanes and, in the home, on frying pans.

SPACECRAFT PROTECTION

To withstand the effects of extreme temperatures and the collisions of meteorites, the spacecraft is protected by various layers that are bonded together with adhesive silicon. The exterior is made of aluminum. Next is a fabric that is resistant to very high temperatures, followed by a fabric to insulate against low temperatures.

HIGH-TEMPERATURE FABRIC
To protect against the harmful effect of the Sun.

LOW-TEMPERATURE FABRIC
To protect against extremely low temperatures

SILICON ADHESIVE

ALUMINUM
protects the spacecraft from meteorite impact.

western union
MCDONNELL DOUGLAS
WESTAR VI
HUGHES
HUGHES AIRCRAFT COMPANY

934095602 98 302 456

BARCODE

provides information via a combination of parallel vertical lines that differ in thickness and spacing. Business and industry use a special scanner to read them.

Global Interconnection

ommunications using satellites have made it possible to connect places that are very far from one another and to bring information to very remote regions. The satellites are primarily in geosynchronous orbits—that is, the satellite orbits in the same time it takes the Earth to rotate. This motion allows for more effective transmission systems, because the satellite is stationary with respect to the Earth's surface. There is a virtual fleet of geosynchronous satellites dedicated to various goals: meteorology, research, navigation, military uses, and, obviously, telecommunications.

Connections

Communication can be established between any two points on Earth. The signals sent and received between terrestrial and satellite antennas are in the radio-wave spectrum, and they range from telephone conversations and television to computer data. A call from Europe to the United States, for example, involves sending a signal to a terrestrial station, which retransmits the signal to a satellite. The satellite then retransmits the signal so that it can be received by an antenna in the United States for transmission to its final destination.

DOWNWARD LINK
The satellite retransmits signals to other points: a downward connection is made.

UPWARD LINK
The satellite captures signals that come from the Earth. An upward connection is made.

Terrestrial Stations

These stations are buildings that house the antennas and all the necessary equipment on land for sending and receiving satellite signals. The buildings can be large structures, and the antennas can act as receivers and transmitters of thousands of streams of information. In other cases, they are small buildings equipped for communications but designed to operate on board ships or airplanes.

TRANSMITTING ANTENNA
The terrestrial antenna receives information from the satellite and retransmits it. This is the key for every kind of telecommunication.

TELEVISION BROADCAST CONNECTIONS
make it possible to transmit the news or other events via satellites that capture the signals and distribute them to different geographic locations.

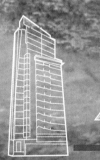

NATIONAL TRANSMISSION GRID
Fixed structure on Earth that communicates with the antenna and receives information

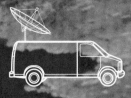

PUBLIC NETWORK
For telephone communication between two points

PRIVATE NETWORK
Groups of private corporations, such as TV networks

PRIVATE
Private clients who pay for satellite access

MOBILE UNIT
Used for covering news or events that occur in different locations

FIXED SENDING AND RECEIVING ANTENNA can target specific places on the Earth.

take the light from the Sun and transform it into electrical energy.

TRANSPONDER This is the heart of the satellite. It corrects for atmosphere-produced distortions of the radio signals.

MOVEMENT ON THREE AXES To correct its position, the satellite turns in three directions: an axis perpendicular to its orbit and the horizontal and vertical axes.

REFLECTOR captures signals and retransmits them directly.

REFLECTOR

Direction to the Earth

PITCH

ROLL

YAW

Velocity Vector

Orbit

CONSTELLATION OF IRIDIUM SATELLITES Iridium is a satellite-based, mobile telephone system in low Earth orbit. It consists of 66 satellites that follow a polar orbit.

TELEPHONE COMMUNICATIONS are possible between an airplane and land by means of satellites.

Area of Maximum Power

Low-Power Boundaries

TELEPHONY CONNECTION A terrestrial antenna receives signals and transmits them to a center that resends to them in the corresponding format.

CENTER/ OPERATOR

SATELLITE FOOTPRINT Transmitted radio waves cover a defined area when they arrive at Earth. The area is known as a footprint.

TV The signal arrives from the center via the antenna.

LAND LINE The voice signal goes from the center to the desired location.

MOBILE TELEPHONES can receive voice and images depending on the signal sent.

Global Satellite Navigation

he Global Positioning System (GPS), developed by the US Department of Defense, makes it possible to determine the position of a person, a vehicle, or a ship anywhere in the world. The GPS system, which uses a constellation of two dozen Navstar satellites, became fully operational in 1995. Although it began as a military initiative, the GPS system was soon extended to commercial applications, which now include handheld navigation systems. A new development called the European Galileo satellite navigation system is now underway. It resembles the GPS system but uses a constellation of 30 satellites. The European system is projected to become fully operational by 2020.

Operation

Based on the electromagnetic waves sent by the satellite, the receivers can convert signals received into position, velocity, and estimated time, because the distance is the product of the velocity and the time. Four satellites are required to calculate the exact position. The first three form an area of triple intersection, while the fourth functions as a checking mechanism. If the area swept out by the fourth satellite does not coincide with the intersection determined by the other three, the position must be corrected.

1 PHASE 1
The first satellite sends its coordinates. The navigation receiver captures a signal, which indicates at what distance the satellite is located and defines a sphere of possible locations.

2 PHASE 2
Using the coordinates of a second satellite, the receiver can determine the user's location as being anywhere along the intersection of the two spheres.

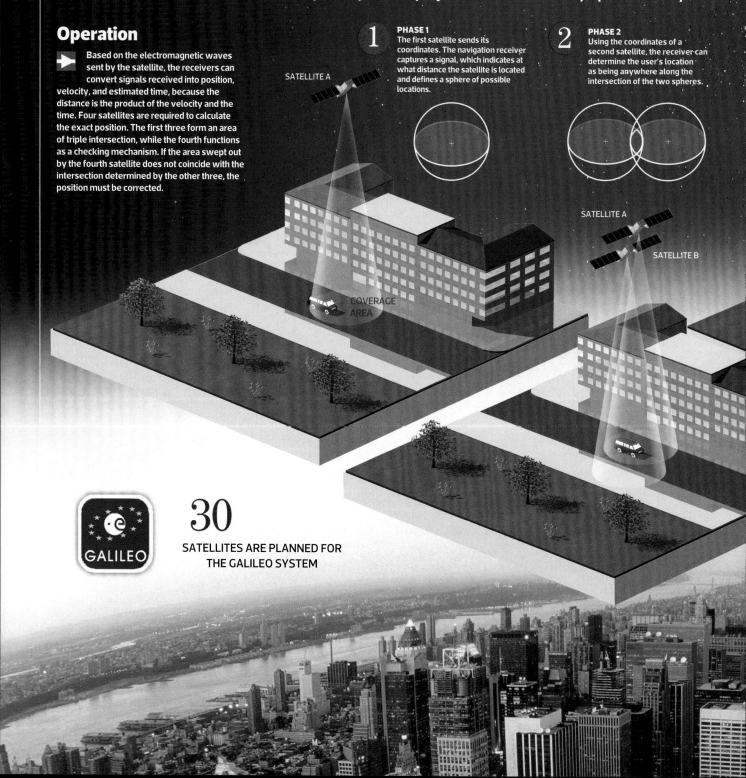

SATELLITE A

COVERAGE AREA

SATELLITE A

SATELLITE B

30
SATELLITES ARE PLANNED FOR THE GALILEO SYSTEM

GALILEO

10 feet (3 m)

TECHNICAL SPECIFICATIONS: GALILEO SATELLITE

First launched	2006
Orbital altitude	14,300 miles (23,000 km)
Orbital period	14 hours
Organization	European Union
Final number in orbit	30 (24 active)

Galileo System

The European Galileo project (which placed its first experimental satellite into orbit in late 2005) is a satellite navigation system that is based on a constellation of 30 satellites (24 operational and 6 spares) in three medium Earth orbits in different planes to ensure global coverage. As with the GPS navigation system, it will permit a variety of applications in addition to navigation, such as the management of taxi fleets in large cities and the ability to locate stolen automobiles or other property. The Galileo project arose in part to gain independence from the GPS system, which could be interrupted or modified to be less accurate if deemed necessary by the US government.

ORBIT ABOUT 55° to the equatorial plane

Equatorial Plane

GALILEO ORBIT
The orbit of the satellites ensures sufficient coverage for calculating precise positions on the Earth.

VELOCITY OF THE WAVES **186,000 miles per second (300,000 km/s)**

ELECTROMAGNETIC WAVES
are sent by the satellite, and from them the receiver determines its location. The waves travel at 186,000 miles per second (300,000 km/s).

SATELLITE A
SATELLITE B
SATELLITE C

3 **PHASE 3**
Combining three satellites allows a common point to be determined to indicate the exact position of the navigator.

4 **PHASE 4**
With a fourth satellite, errors in the determined position introduced by inaccuracies in the receiver's clock can be corrected.

SATELLITE A
SATELLITE B
SATELLITE C
SATELLITE D

THE RECEIVER
has all the controls necessary to specify the location of a certain point. These indicate to the observer all the desired coordinates.

RECEIVING LOCATION

INDICATOR
For latitude, altitude, and longitude

CONTROL
For navigating through the displayed map

Environmental Satellites

U nder the guidance of the French Space agency CNES, Spot 1 was put into orbit in 1986; it was the first satellite of what is today a satellite constellation that can take very high-resolution photographs of Earth. The latest version, Spot 7, was launched in 2014 . Today, it is considered a commercial satellite par excellence, used by companies in the oil and agricultural industries. The United States, in turn, launched Landsat in 1972, the latest version of which has been launched in 2017. ●

Spot 7 Capabilities

The development of the Spot satellite constellation made it possible to commercially offer photographic monitoring of events linked to the environment. The latest version, the SPOT 7, has two NAOMI (New AstroSat Optical Modular Instrument) cameras capable of obtaining a resolution of 7.2 feet (2.2 m) in panchromatic mode, a resolution that rises to 4.9 feet (1.5 m) after being processed. Each image occupies a width of 37 mi (60 km). The constellation formed by the SPOT 6 and SPOT 7 satellites is able to photograph about six million square kilometers of the Earth's surface per day and works in coordination with the two French Pleiades observing satellites.

SPOT SATELLITES
They work together, thanks to which it is possible to obtain an image from any point of the globe daily.

TECHNICAL SPECIFICATIONS

Launch date	Jun 30, 2014
Orbital altitude	407 miles (655 km)
Orbital period	98.79 minutes
Maximum resolution	4.9 feet (1.5 m)
Organization	Airbus Defence & Space

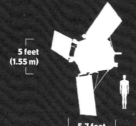

5 feet (1.55 m)

5.7 feet (1.75 m)

US Satellite

Landstat 8 has two terrestrial observing instruments: the Operational Land Imager (OLI) and the Thermal Infrared Sensor (TIRS). OLI and TIRS will collect the data together to provide coincident images of the Earth's surface. It will be located in a heliosynchronous polar orbit 438 mi (705 km) high with a slope of 98.2°. From this orbit you can observe the entire surface of the Earth every 16 days.

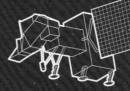

LANDSAT 8
built by Orbital Sciences Corporation in Gilbert, Arizona, has a shelf life of 5 years, but carries enough fuel for 10 years of operations.

MARCH

FEBRUARY

JANUARY

DECEMBER

NOVEMBER

SEPTEMBER

OCTOBER

HELIOSYNCHRONOUS ORBIT

In order to compare observations of a given point captured on different dates, the images must be taken under similar light conditions. To this end, a Sun-synchronous orbit is used, which means it is possible to view the entire Earth's surface for a period of 26 days.

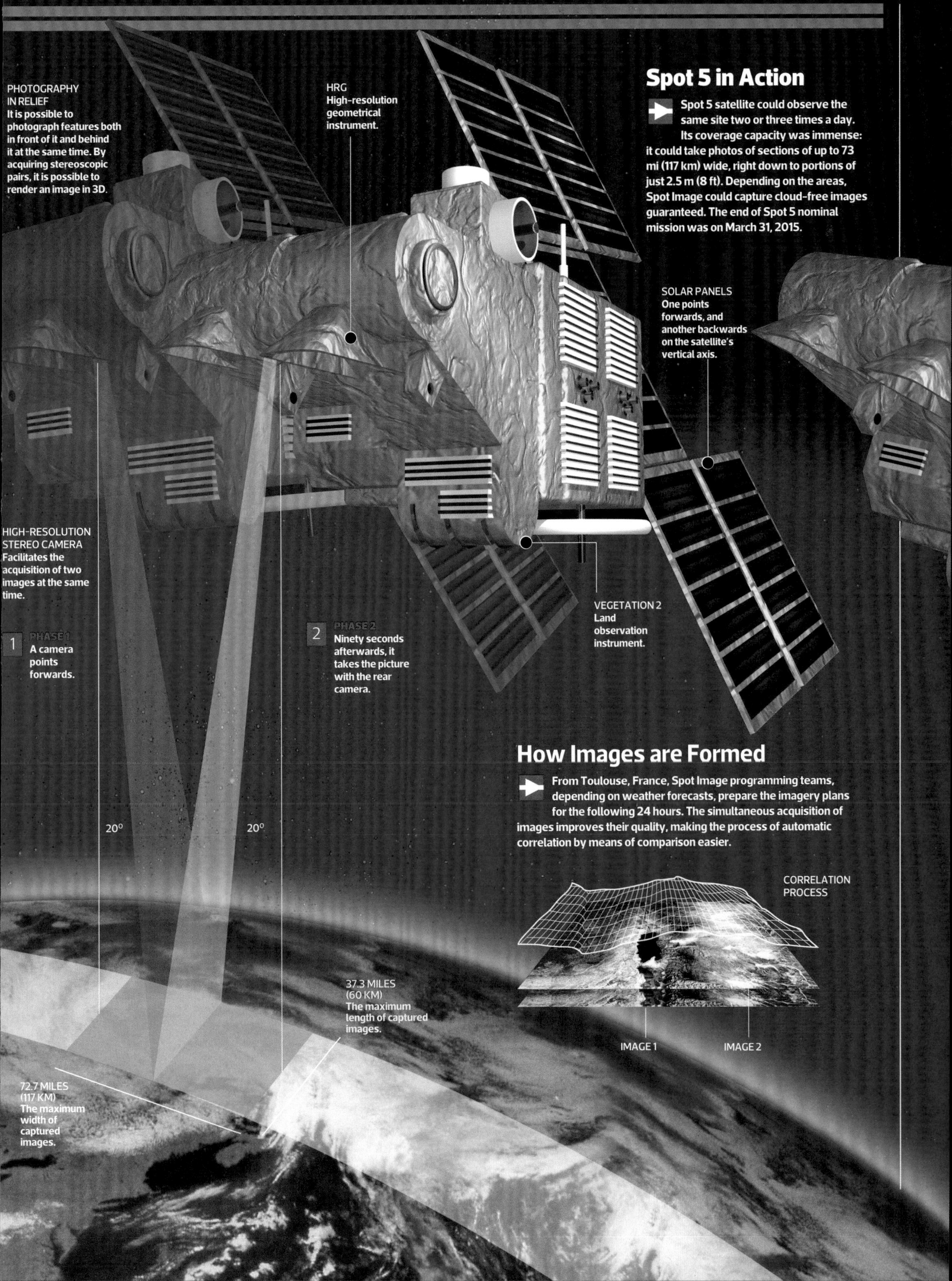

PHOTOGRAPHY IN RELIEF
It is possible to photograph features both in front of it and behind it at the same time. By acquiring stereoscopic pairs, it is possible to render an image in 3D.

HRG
High-resolution geometrical instrument.

Spot 5 in Action

Spot 5 satellite could observe the same site two or three times a day. Its coverage capacity was immense: it could take photos of sections of up to 73 mi (117 km) wide, right down to portions of just 2.5 m (8 ft). Depending on the areas, Spot Image could capture cloud-free images guaranteed. The end of Spot 5 nominal mission was on March 31, 2015.

SOLAR PANELS
One points forwards, and another backwards on the satellite's vertical axis.

HIGH-RESOLUTION STEREO CAMERA
Facilitates the acquisition of two images at the same time.

1 PHASE 1
A camera points forwards.

2 PHASE 2
Ninety seconds afterwards, it takes the picture with the rear camera.

VEGETATION 2
Land observation instrument.

20°   20°

How Images are Formed

From Toulouse, France, Spot Image programming teams, depending on weather forecasts, prepare the imagery plans for the following 24 hours. The simultaneous acquisition of images improves their quality, making the process of automatic correlation by means of comparison easier.

CORRELATION PROCESS

37.3 MILES (60 KM)
The maximum length of captured images.

72.7 MILES (117 KM)
The maximum width of captured images.

IMAGE 1   IMAGE 2

From the Air

hotographs taken by Spot 5 can show the geography of any region of the world in different scales, from images of 8 feet (2.5 m) on Earth to fringe areas 37 miles (60 km) wide. Spot 5's high-definition capacity makes in-depth close-ups possible: it can target very specific places, from areas of vegetation to harbors, oceans, geographic borders, and forest-fire zones. Here Israel and its border regions—with Syria, Lebanon, and Egypt—together with the Dead Sea and the Golan Heights were photographed by the satellite, offering a panoramic image with significant detail.

ISRAEL

Latitude 32.98º
Longitude 35.57º

Surface area	8,019 square miles (20,769 sq km)
Population	8,174,527 (2016)
Population density	755 per square mile (302/sq km)
Capital	Jerusalem
Currency	Shekel

1,400 square (3,600 sq km) miles

The maximum surface area attainable by Spot 5 photos. It can do so both on local scales (for which finer resolution is used) and on regional scales.

THE DEAD SEA AS TAKEN BY LANDSAT 7

The North American satellite took this photograph of the Dead Sea in February 1975. The image combines optical and infrared techniques (in this wavelength range, water is seen as black). The Dead Sea is in the center, between Israel (on the left) and Jordan (on the right). North is up.

The Dead Sea is the lowest body of water in the world, 1,300 feet (400 m) below sea level. Its water evaporates rapidly in the desert climate, leaving behind dissolved minerals.

The surface of the desert appears brown.

The vegetation is seen in green.

Syria

SEA OF GALILEE

Nazareth

Haifa

JORDAN RIVER

DEAD SEA

The West Bank

Its desert characteristics are observable in the color photograph taken by Spot 5.

THE JUDEAN DESERT

The image shows different elevations and terrain with significant detail.

The region of Sodom, 1,270 feet (387 m) below sea level, is the lowest place on the planet.

Jerusalem

Tel Aviv

Israel

Gaza

EAN SEA

Image Resolution

Technological developments have permitted increased resolution of what is called the image capture of geographic space. The maximum definition possible is 8 feet (2.5 m) on the Earth's surface. In some cases it is better to use resolutions of 16, 32, and 66 feet (5, 10, and 20 m). The pictures provided by Spot can cover an areas as much as 37 miles (60 km) wide and can be used for checking harvests, evaluating natural catastrophes, and checking demographic growth.

Satellite	Size of the pixel	Image
Spot 1 to 3	32 feet (10 m)	Color and B&W
	66 feet (20 m)	Color
Spot 4	16 feet (5 m)	Color and B&W
	32 feet (10 m)	Color
Spot 5	8 feet (2.5 m)	Color or B&W
	16 feet (5 m)	Color or B&W
	32 feet (10 m)	Color or B&W

3-D images

Spot 5's scanning method makes it possible to construct images (primarily topographical relief) in three dimensions

8 feet (2.5 m)

Is the finest resolution attainable by the Spot 5 satellite and is capable of showing the details of a ship in a port.

Jordan

Egypt

0 miles   6
(km)   (10)

A Different Vacation

P erhaps a few years from now traveling to the edge of space will be another option for a vacation. Right now various private enterprises already have plans to offer this type of recreation. In April 2001, an American businessman, Dennis Tito, made a successful trip to the International Space Station. The first commercial space traveler, he paid $20 million dollars for an eight-day stay. One year later, the Australian Mark Shuttleworth did the same. Then came the formation of SpaceShipOne, which has the potential of allowing thousands of tourists to travel to space at moderate cost.

DENNIS TITO

Altitude in km (miles)

100 (62) MAXIMUM ALTITUDE
The spacecraft reaches an altitude of 62 miles (100 km) before falling back into the atmosphere. The members of the crew experience microgravity for six minutes.

90 (56)

80 (50)

70 (45)

60 (37) THE ENGINE
fires for 80 seconds, and the craft reaches a velocity of 2,225 miles per hour (3,580 k/h).

50 (31)

40 (25) LIFTOFF
After one hour of flight—and at an altitude of 9.5 miles (15.24 km)—the launching aircraft White Knight releases SpaceShipOne.

30 (19)

115 feet (35 m)

270 feet (82 m)

TECHNICAL SPECIFICATIONS: WHITE KNIGHT

Launch date	**June 2004**
Maximum altitude	**9.5 miles (15.24 km)**
First pilot	**Mike Melvill**
Enterprise	**Private**

The Voyage

Suborbital flights are less expensive than orbital flights. The voyage typically lasts about two hours at a maximum velocity of 2,225 miles per hour (3,580 km/h) and a maximum altitude of approximately 60 miles (100 km). The stay in outer space lasts only a few minutes, during which time the traveler can see the beautiful profile of the Earth and experience the effects of microgravity. Such flights are available to paying passengers.

REENTRY
The pilot configures the descent.

GLIDING
SpaceShipOne descends toward the ground.

LANDING
The White Knight returns for a landing.

$200,000
APPROXIMATE COST OF A SUBORBITAL FLIGHT

4 days
OF TRAINING

2 hours
FLIGHT DURATION

TECHNICAL SPECIFICATIONS:
SPACESHIPONE

Date of launch	June 2004
Maximum altitude	about 62 miles (100 km)
First pilot	Mike Melvill
Enterprise	Private

16 feet
(5 m)

49 feet
(15 m)

WEIGHT OF
THE SPACESHIP

8,100 pounds
(3,670 kg)

The Cockpit

Equipped with advanced technology that permits the pilot to maneuver the spacecraft safely. It has 16 circular glass panes for a panoramic view of space and the Earth below. A central stick and rudder pedals are the principal controls the pilot uses when it is time for the spacecraft to fly.

THE CREW
Equipped with pressurized suits. The crew is trained for the flight and sits at the rear of the craft.

BOOSTER
Solid hybrid rocket engine

ENGINE
FRAME
With liquid
fuel

THRUSTERS
allow the craft to
ascend or descend
during the flight.

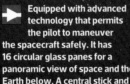

RUDDERS
Activated
electronically, they
lend more strength
to spaceflight.

AILERONS
Used for
controlling
the airplane's
altitude

MOVEMENT
OF THE NOSE
From side to
side around the
center of gravity

FEATHERING
The wings
pivot upward to
allow for safe
reentry.

CIRCULAR PANES
There are 16 glass panes
that provide structural
integrity to the fuselage.

ALTITUDE
DIRECTOR
Used for reentry
into the atmosphere

RUDDER PEDALS
They are used for
banking to prevent
side-to-side motion

EXHIBITOR
shows the position of
the craft with respect to
the Earth, the route to
its destination, and the
compression of the
air on the wings.

CENTRAL
CONTROL STICK
It controls the
craft's pitch.

ENGINE
The engine is
started with
push-buttons
and burns fuel
for 65 seconds.

REGULATOR
checks for deviations
from the trajectory.

N328KF

Glossary

Antenna

Dish or mast for receiving or sending radio signals.

Applications Satellite

Type of unmanned satellite for commercial use and for scientists who study the Earth. Application satellites can be broadly classified as communications, environmental, or navigational.

Artificial Intelligence

In general, the capacity of a machine to act like an intelligent being.

Astronaut

Person sent into space. To be able to perform tasks in space, astronauts wear pressurized suits. The training program is difficult and exhaustive.

Astronautics

Science that studies the design, construction, and function of spacecraft and the problems related to interplanetary space navigation. It also refers to related technologies.

Booster Rocket

Rocket that is attached to a primary rocket to increase thrust at liftoff.

Console

Instrument panel with controls and displays. The space shuttle contains a command console in the flight deck.

Depressurized

To remove or lose the air pressure within an enclosed area. For example, air locks are depressurized when astronauts in space suits prepare to exit the lock and leave the spacecraft.

Digital Signal

A signal that provides information numerically, such as a series of on-off values. Computers use digital signals that are typically represented by electric signals formed by a series of high or low voltage levels. Digital electronic equipment represents continually varying (analog) information as a series of discrete values.

Docking Adapter

The part of the spacecraft designed to join with another spacecraft when they are docked together.

Docking Port

A door that can be opened between two docked spacecraft so that the members of the crew can move from one to the other.

Energy Matrix

Also known as the solar matrix, it provides electric energy to the ionic motor of the spacecraft. They are less expensive than solar panels and also more resistant to space radiation.

Environmental Satellites

Satellites that gather environmental information about the Earth, such as images of the storms in the atmosphere, ocean temperatures and currents, and snow and ice cover. Images of the Earth's surface in different wavelengths can help evaluate the composition of rocks and the health of crops and other vegetation.

ESA

European Space Agency. It was established on May 31, 1975, with its principal headquarters in Paris.

Fuel

Substance that burns to provide energy. Some types of rocket fuel are liquid; other types are solid or rubbery. Rocket fuel burns with an oxidizer, producing gases that are expelled through the nozzles to provide thrust. Rockets carry their own oxidizer so that they burn fuel and provide propulsion in outer space, where there is no air.

Helmet

A space-suit helmet is made of strong plastic. The helmet contains a valve to let in oxygen and remove carbon dioxide. The helmet is airtight and contains communication gear, such as a microphone and headphones.

Image Spectrometer

Image spectrometer is a type of camera that records a digital image in two or more specific wavelengths, such as infrared and ultraviolet. The images can then be evaluated to obtain information about materials, such as the composition of rocks in an image of the Earth's surface.

Infrared Radiation

Light with wavelengths somewhat longer than those of red light in the visible spectrum. It is invisible to the human eye. Infrared light can be readily used for transmitting information between two devices that are in close proximity to each other without their having to be connected by cables. Infrared radiation requires less energy to produce than visible light and does not interfere with light.

Laser

Device that produces coherent light—that is, light composed of a single wavelength and in phase with each other. Lasers can be built from a variety of substances (such as ruby and certain gases), which are then stimulated electrically to produce a laser beam. Laser beams can have many uses. Intense beams can cut materials with great precision. Laser light is also used for transmitting digital information, because it can be readily generated in very short pulses.

Life-Support System

Equipment that provides air, water, and heat so that the astronauts can live in space.

Lock

Chamber of the spacecraft with an interior door connecting the cabin to another, outside door that opens into space. The members of he crew typically put their space suits on in he lock. If they did not use the lock, all the air rom the spacecraft would escape.

Lunar Vehicle

Battery-powered vehicle used to drive over he lunar surface.

Manned Maneuvering Unit

Apparatus that astronauts formerly used to perform work, such as capturing satellites and testing new equipment, outside the spacecraft. It consisted of a framework with small directional thrusters.

Mariner

A series of US space probes for the study of the interior planets of the solar system (Mercury, Venus, Mars). None was designed to land on a planet. In spite of the relative limitations of these missions compared to later probes, they contributed important planetary information that was used for later, more complex missions, such as the Viking.

Mars Pathfinder

US space probe that successfully landed on Mars on July 4, 1997, in the area called es Vallis.

Messages from the Earth

Space probes on missions that carry them beyond the solar system have carried messages from the Earth to possible extraterrestrials who might find them. Discs and plates have been used to record information about the Earth and its life-forms with maps, images, and sounds.

Microelectronics

Miniaturized semiconductor electronic circuits have revolutionized spacecraft systems from control and navigation to communications.

Microgravity

The condition in which objects experience no or virtually no gravitational effects. It is associated with weightlessness. Many experiments conducted by astronauts in space take advantage of the microgravity in orbit. Some such experiments concern creating new types of materials; others involve studying the effects of microgravity on plants or other living things.

Mission Control

Facility of a space agency for monitoring and controlling a spaceflight.

NASA

National Aeronautics and Space Administration, the US organization in charge of space exploration. Its headquarters are in Washington, D.C. NASA was created in 1958 by President Dwight D. Eisenhower.

Navigation Systems

Traditional systems of spacecraft navigation tracked the spacecraft from the ground and depended on human controllers there. In modern autonomous navigation systems, the path of the spacecraft is calculated and corrected using images of the asteroids and stars taken by an onboard camera system, then combining the information with the navigation system.

Operations Center

The operations center of mission control that monitors spaceflights using telemetry technology, which allows technical aspects to be monitored in real time.

Opportunity

The second of two NASA rovers that landed on the surface of Mars in 2004.

Orbital Perturbations

There are many subtle effects that perturb the orbits of Earth satellites. Some of the factors are the asymmetry of the Earth's orbit, solar and lunar effects, atmospheric influences, and pressure from solar radiation.

Oxidizer

Chemical agent (normally a gas) that is burned together with the fuel to fire the rocket engine.

Parachute

A device made of a strong textile that opens up in the shape of a huge umbrella, used to slow the fall of astronauts or rockets.

Payload

Materials or scientific instruments transported into space by a manned or unmanned spacecraft that are not part of the launch vehicle itself.

Pressure Suit

An airtight, inflatable suit designed to protect the body from low pressure at high altitude or in space. A space suit is a type of pressure suit.

Propulsion System

The most common propulsion system used for rockets is chemical, driven by combustion. A chemical rocket engine carries both a fuel and an oxidizer, which together take up most of the volume of the rocket. The fuel burns when it is combined with the oxidizer, and the escaping gases produce the propulsion. Other types of rocket propulsion systems include the ion (electric) system in which electrically accelerated ions are discharged from the engine to produce thrust.

Radar

A system that emits radio waves and detects any echoes of those same waves. Given that radio waves travel at the velocity of light, the times involved can be very brief. Among the uses of radar are measuring distances, planet cartography, and the study of meteorology. A type of radar called Doppler radar can be used to determine the speed of moving objects that reflect the radio waves.

Reaction Control System

The propulsion system used to change the position of a spacecraft.

Reentry

The portion of spaceflight in which the spacecraft enters the atmosphere to return to Earth. As the spacecraft passes through the atmosphere, the friction between the air molecules and the spacecraft causes intense heating. Therefore, the surface of the spacecraft is protected by a thermal shield constructed of plastic, metal, and ceramics. Some materials are designed to vaporize, dissipating the heat without harming the spacecraft or its crew.

Rescue Ball

The rescue ball was designed to help crew members without pressurized suits escape. It is made of space suit material and has an oxygen supply so that an astronaut could escape safely to another ship.

Robotic Manipulation System

Robotic arm installed in the space shuttle, used for tasks such as unloading the space shuttle's payload bay.

Robotics

Technology that designs machines capable of independently carrying out a number of tasks and adapting their actions to the requirements of the moment.

Rocket

Reaction engine that carries its own fuel and a source of oxygen so that it can function in space as well as in the atmosphere. It is driven by gases that exit from nozzles. Launch vehicles consist of various rocket stages and can make use of booster rockets. A rocket produces the kinetic energy necessary to send objects (such as manned spacecraft, artificial satellites, and space probes) into space. The most common type of rockets are chemical rockets, which may use liquid or solid fuels and oxidizers.

Satellite

Object that orbits a much larger object. Artificial satellites do not carry a crew. They orbit the Earth and carry out such functions as the transmission of telephone calls or information about meteorology.

Scientific Satellites

These compile information and carry out exact studies of the Sun, other stars, the Earth, and the space environment. Such satellites can gather data that cannot be obtained on the surface of the Earth because of the Earth's atmosphere.

Sensor

Device commonly used in scientific and other types of instruments aboard spacecraft for gathering data and information.

Solar Panel

Panel covered with solar cells. The cells collect sunlight and convert it into electricity, which can be used to operate the equipment within a spacecraft.

Soyuz

Series of both manned and unmanned Soviet and Russian spacecraft. The Soyuz replaced the Vostok in the mid-1970s. The Russians use new versions of the Soyuz for launchings to the International Space Station. The original Soyuz series of spacecraft was developed between 1967 and 1981 and was used for 41 launches. These capsules were replaced by the more modern Soyuz-T, launched 15 times between 1980 and 1986. The most recent generation is the Soyuz-TM, the first of which was launched in 1986.

Space Blanket

Layer of powdered metal on a plastic film applied as spacecraft insulation or to reflect radio signals. Blankets made of this material retain 80 percent of the body's heat.

Space Exploration

The era of space exploration began in 1957 with the launching of the first artificial satellite. From that time, many astronauts and robot craft have left the Earth to explore space. Twelve astronauts have even landed on the Moon. Space probes equipped with automatic instruments have visited many bodies of the solar system, including comets and asteroids as well as the planets and their moons.

Space Junk

Any artificial object orbiting the Earth in space that has no purpose. It includes such materials as big rocket fragments and small particles of paint. Space junk has been accumulating since the beginning of space exploration.

Space Missions

Space missions are organized by a number of space-exploration agencies, including NASA, the European Space Agency, and the Russian Space Agency. Spacecraft can be manned or unmanned. Voyages are planned years in advance. International teams construct rockets, satellites, and probes that carry out specific tasks, such as visiting a planet or constructing the International Space Station. Some spacecraft are part of a series, such as the Apollo lunar mission.

Space Probe

Unmanned spacecraft sent to gather information from planets and other bodies of the solar system. Some probes are limited to flying close to a planet. At a preset distance, the instruments are activated to record data. When the probe leaves the planet behind, the instruments are deactivated. Many probes have been sent to land on the surface of a body of the solar system. Such probes have been used to land on the Moon, Venus, Mars, and Saturn's moon Titan.

Space Shuttle

The first spacecraft capable of returning to the Earth on its own and being reused on multiple missions. Today the US fleet has three shuttles: *Discovery*, *Atlantis*, and *Endeavour*. The *Challenger* and *Columbia* were both destroyed in accidents (in 1986 and 2003, respectively).

Space Station

A base designed to orbit the Earth for a long period of time. Crew members can live nd work in the space station for several months.

Space Suit

 suit that allows the wearer to survive in pace. It protects against too much or too little ressure and harmful radiation, and it also rovides the oxygen necessary for breathing.

Space Tourism

ecreational space travel, which first came bout as a project launched in August 1999 etween the Space Adventures enterprise of ne United States and a Russian entity. In April 001 the American businessman Dennis Tito aid $20 million for a trip to the International pace Station as the first space tourist.

Space Underwear

efore astronauts put on a space suit, they put n an apparatus for collecting urine that has a ube going to a receptacle. Women wear short ants, which absorb the urine and conduct it to ne receptacle. They also wear underclothes quipped with tubes of water to cool the stronaut.

Spacelab

pacelab was the space station designed o fit within the payload bay of the space huttle. The Spacelab project was begun vith a 1973 agreement between the United tates and the nations belonging to the SA. The first flight occurred in November 983. The Spacelab was lifted into space or the last time in November 1997, when ne development of the International Space tation began.

Spirit

ne of two robots—the other being Opportunity—that was launched in 2003 rom Earth and that landed on Mars in 2004. hey carefully explored the surface of the lanet. Both vehicles are part of the NASA Mars Exploration Rovers mission. They have ools that allow them to gather rocks and ake soil samples to be analyzed for chemical omposition. The robots are located on pposite sides of the Red Planet so that they

can photographically study very different places.

Sputnik

Satellite that inaugurated the age of space exploration. Sputnik 1, launched in 1957, was an aluminum sphere 23 inches (58 cm) in diameter. Its instrumentation sent back information about cosmic radiation, meteorites, and the density and temperature of the Earth's upper atmosphere for 21 days. Sputnik 2 was the first to lift a living being, the dog Laika, into space.

Suborbital Flights

Flight designed to reach space but not achieve orbit. A typical suborbital flight lasts about two hours and reaches a speed of 2,220 miles per hour (3,580 km/h) and an altitude of about 62 miles (100 km). The time spent in space lasts only a few minutes.

Telescope

Instrument for magnifying the image of distant objects. Astronomical telescopes are used for observing the stars, planets, and other celestial bodies. The term is used to refer to instruments that magnify an optical image or an image produced by other types of electromagnetic radiation, such as radio waves. The Hubble Space Telescope is an orbiting telescope that can make observations free from the distorting effects of the atmosphere.

Thermal Insulator

Material that conducts heat poorly. It is used to protect the walls of a rocket from the high temperatures produced by burning fuel and to protect the skin of a spacecraft from the heat produced by air friction during reentry into the atmosphere.

Training

The astronaut training program takes several months. Regardless of educational background, trainees must study mathematics, meteorology, astronomy, physics, and space navigation. They regularly work in flight simulators and receive training in the use of the

spacecraft computers and other equipment.

Viking

NASA sent the Viking 1 and Viking 2 probes to Mars in 1975. Both probes landed on the planet and carried out observations from its surface.

Vostok

Soviet space program that put a total of six cosmonauts into orbit around the Earth between April 1961 and June 1963. The first astronaut to orbit the Earth—at an altitude of 195 miles (315 km)—was Yury Gagarin, the only crew member of the Vostok 1.

Voyager 1 and 2

The space probes Voyager 1 and 2 were sent by NASA to study the outer solar system. Voyager 1 was launched in 1977, passed Jupiter in 1979, and passed Saturn in 1980. Voyager 2 was also launched in 1977; it passed by Jupiter and Saturn to reach Uranus in 1986 and Neptune in 1989. Both probes are heading out of the solar system and have provided data about the far reaches of the solar system.

X-rays

In November 1895 William Roentgen, when studying the production of electron beams known as cathode rays, became aware of a mysterious type of radiation that had not been observed before, and he called it X-rays. Astronomy has been strongly influenced by Roentgen's discovery in spite of the fact that X-rays coming from celestial objects cannot penetrate the Earth's atmosphere.

For More Information

Association of Science – Technology Centers

818 Connecticut Avenue, NW

7th Floor

Washington, DC 20006-2734

(202) 783-7200

Website: www.astc.org

Through strategic alliances and global partnerships, the Association of Science-Technology Centers (ASTC) strives to increase awareness of the valuable contributions its members make to their communities and the field of informal STEM learning.

Canada Science and Technology Museum

PO Box 9724, Station T

Ottawa, Ontario K1G 5A3

Canada

(866) 442-4416

Website: cstmuseum.techno-science.ca

The Canada Science and Technology Museum is the largest of its kind in Canada, and fulfills its mission through its collection, its permanent, temporary and traveling exhibitions, as well as special events, school programs, and workshops.

H. R. MacMillan Space Centre

1100 Chestnut Street (Vanier Park)

Vancouver, British Columbia V6J 3J9

Canada

(604) 738-7827

Website: www.spacecentre.ca/

The H. R. MacMillan Space Centre is a nonprofit community resource. Through innovative programming, exhibits, and activities, the centre's goal is to educate, inspire and evoke a sense of wonder about the universe, our planet, and space exploration.

Kennedy Space Center

Kennedy Space Center Visitor Complex

SR 405

Titusville, FL 32899

(877) 404-3769

Website: www.kennedyspacecenter.com

Kennedy Space Center Visitor Complex is organized into Mission Zones where attractions and tours are grouped by chronological era. From the dawn of space exploration to current and ongoing missions, you can get an up-close, hands-on feel for the story of humans in space.

Liberty Science Center

Liberty State Park 222

Jersey City Boulevard

Jersey City, NJ 07305

(201) 200-1000

Website: www.lsc.org

Liberty Science Center is a 300,000-square-foot learning center dedicated to bringing the excitement of science to people of all ages.

Rose Center for Earth and Space – American Museum of Natural History

175-208 79th Street Central Park West

New York, NY 10024

(212) 769-15100

Website: www.amnh.org/exhibitions/permanent-exhibitions/rose-center-for-earth-and-space

The Rose Center for Earth and Space encompasses the spectacular Hayden Sphere and exhibitions that explore the vast range of sizes in the cosmos, the 13-billion-year history of the universe, the nature of galaxies, stars, and planets, and the dynamic features of planet Earth.

Websites

Because of the changing nature of internet links, Rosen Publishing has developed an online list of websites related to the subject of this book. This site is updated regularly. Please use this link to access the list:

http://www.rosenlinks.com/VES/space

Further Reading

Dickinson, Terence. *Hubble's Universe: Greatest Discoveries and Latest Images*. Ontario, Canada: Firefly Books, 2014.

DK Publishing. *Space!* New York, NY: DK Publishing, 2015.

DK Publishing. *Space Exploration*. New York, NY: DK Publishing, 2014.

Gilliland, Ben. *How to Build a Universe: From the Big Bang to the End of the Universe*. New York, NY: Sterling, 2015.

Miller, Ron. *Spaceships: An Illustrated History of the Real and the Imagined*. Washington, DC: Smithsonian Books, 2016.

Sagan, Carl. *Cosmos*. New York, NY: Ballantine Books, 2013.

Schilling, Govert. *Deep Space: Beyond the Solar System to the End of the Universe and the Beginning of Time*. New York, NY: Black Dog and Leventhal Publishers, 2014.

Shetterly, Margot Lee. *Hidden Figures: The American Dream and the Untold Story of the Black Women Mathematicians Who Helped Win the Space Race*. New York, NY: HarperCollins Publishers, 2016.

Smith, Robert W., and David H. Devorkin. *The Hubble Cosmos: 25 Years of New Vistas in Space*. Washington, DC: National Geographic, 2015.

Snedden, Robert. *A Brief Illustrated History of Space Exploration*. North Mankato, MN: Capstone Press, 2017.

Index